About This Book

Why is this topic important?

Almost everywhere, it seems, people are being asked to do more with less. Training professionals are no exception. They have less time and fewer resources, while the demand for new knowledge and skills grows at an ever-increasing pace. Whether it's a quicker way to determine learning needs or worksheets that can shorten the training design phase, trainers need low-cost, ready-to-use tools that speed up the training process.

What can you achieve with this book?

There's no reason ever to be stuck looking for a training tool again. Veteran trainer Jane Bozarth brings you over one hundred tools that anyone, from the interested manager to the experienced training professional, can turn to when designing or delivering training. Built from contributions by expert practitioners, this book provides dozens of tools of the trade: worksheets for assessing training needs and writing goals and objectives; checklists for organizing the venue; tools for analysis and structuring content; and instant evaluation surveys, which can be customized freely from the accompanying CD. Along with a plethora of worksheets, charts, lists, and outlines, the editor and contributors provide tips for issues such as the effective use of props, staying energized, marketing training programs, and other things they don't tell you in train-the-trainer courses.

How is this book organized?

The tools are organized by chapter into the phases of the "ADDIE" (Analyze, Design, Develop, Implement, Evaluate) model of instructional design. This provides both a familiar format and easy access to material for those needing a tool in a hurry. An accompanying CD includes printable, editable versions of the tools, worksheets, and checklists contained in the book.

About Pfeiffer

Pfeiffer serves the professional development and hands-on resource needs of training and human resource practitioners and gives them products to do their jobs better. We deliver proven ideas and solutions from experts in HR development and HR management, and we offer effective and customizable tools to improve workplace performance. From novice to seasoned professional, Pfeiffer is the source you can trust to make yourself and your organization more successful.

Essential Knowledge Pfeiffer produces insightful, practical, and comprehensive materials on topics that matter the most to training and HR professionals. Our Essential Knowledge resources translate the expertise of seasoned professionals into practical, how-to guidance on critical workplace issues and problems. These resources are supported by case studies, worksheets, and job aids and are frequently supplemented with CD-ROMs, websites, and other means of making the content easier to read, understand, and use.

Essential Tools Pfeiffer's Essential Tools resources save time and expense by offering proven, ready-to-use materials—including exercises, activities, games, instruments, and assessments—for use during a training or team-learning event. These resources are frequently offered in looseleaf or CD-ROM format to facilitate copying and customization of the material.

Pfeiffer also recognizes the remarkable power of new technologies in expanding the reach and effectiveness of training. While e-hype has often created whizbang solutions in search of a problem, we are dedicated to bringing convenience and enhancements to proven training solutions. All our e-tools comply with rigorous functionality standards. The most appropriate technology wrapped around essential content yields the perfect solution for today's on-the-go trainers and human resource professionals.

www.pfeiffer.com

Essential resources for training and HR professionals

For all the members of the NC Trainers' Network Team (TNT), especially those who have given so much more than they've taken.

From **Analysis to Evaluation**

Tools, Tips, and Techniques for Trainers

JANE BOZARTH, Editor

Pfeiffer
A Wiley Imprint
www.pfeiffer.com

Published by Pfeiffer
An Imprint of Wiley
989 Market Street, San Francisco, CA 94103-1741
www.pfeiffer.com

For additional copies/bulk purchases of this book in the U.S. please contact 800-274-4434.

Pfeiffer books and products are available through most bookstores. To contact Pfeiffer directly call our Customer Care Department within the U.S. at 800-274-4434, outside the U.S. at 317-572-3985, fax 317-572-4002, or visit www.pfeiffer.com.

Pfeiffer also publishes its books in a variety of electronic formats. Some content that appears in print may not be available in electronic books.

Library of Congress Cataloging-in-Publication Data

From analysis to evaluation: tools, tips, and techniques for trainers / Jane Bozarth, editor.
   p.   cm.
Includes bibliographical references and index.
ISBN-13: 978-0-7879-8201-0 (pbk.)
   1. Employees—Training of.   I. Bozarth, Jane.-
HF5549.5.T7F697 2008
658.3'124—dc22

2007045004

Acquiring Editor: Lisa Shannon
Director of Development: Kathleen Dolan Davies
Production Editor: Dawn Kilgore

Editor: Rebecca Taff
Editorial Assistant: Marisa Kelley
Manufacturing Supervisor: Becky Morgan

Printed in the United States of America
Printing   10 9 8 7 6 5 4 3 2 1

CONTENTS

CHAPTER 2
Design   51

CHAPTER 3
Develop   **111**

CHAPTER 4

Implement   **185**

CHAPTER 5
Evaluate **239**

CONTENTS OF THE CD-ROM

ACKNOWLEDGMENTS

This book was a special challenge because of the sheer number of contributions, communications, and permission forms and other assorted bureaucracies. My deepest gratitude to the many who contributed their own original materials, especially those authors who were willing to share new items now, rather than save them for their own publications later.

Many thanks for all the support from the usual suspects, those phenomenal trainers from the NC Trainers' Network Team (TNT). Thanks as well to my extended training family: Jennifer Hofmann, Patti Shank, Kassy LaBorie, Karl Kapp, and Nanette Miner. While it is always dangerous to single people out, I would like to note the extraordinary generosity of Jerry Linnins, Jennifer Hofmann, Nanette Miner, Susan Boyd, and Karl Kapp for their help with this project. Reviewers Chopeta Lyons and Lenn Millbower offered many helpful suggestions for the final draft and ended up contributing items of their own. Thanks to Pfeiffer's Martin Delahoussaye for entrusting this project to me, to Susan Rachmeler for her help with development, and to Lisa Shannon for keeping me entertained, even though she wasn't even working on this book. As ever, many thanks to Thom Wright and Ann Gillen Cobb for their support of my many pursuits, some of which occasionally coincide with my job.

Finally, and it is not enough: very special thanks to my dear husband Kent Underwood for continuing to think that it is more cool than annoying to have an author for a wife.

ll true U.S. Southerners—and I am one—know the best recipes are found in what are known as "church cookbooks." Popular fundraising items, church cookbooks are compilations of the congregation members' best efforts. Every contribution obviously can't be entirely original—the number of chicken casserole recipes alone is simply staggering—but are often adaptations from and improvements on other efforts.

The best thing about church cookbooks is that they represent the tried-and-true: contributors don't want to hear that a recipe flopped or was disliked by the cook's family. Over time, original recipes clipped from magazines and food can labels, found to be lacking in flavor, are enhanced; those deemed too complicated are streamlined. So the recipes that end up in the cookbooks are the sure-fire efforts, the ones that have been tweaked to perfection, the ones any cook will proudly share with another. Need a recipe for a chocolate pie? Turn to a church cookbook and you'll find the last word, and on three types: cream, fudge, and chess. Same with spaghetti sauce . . . And meat loaf.

So here's the "church cookbook" for trainers. We've asked training practitioners to share tools they actually use in practice, in the formats they've found useful. Items described as "tools"—such as worksheets, checklists, or templates—are also included on the CD that accompanies the book, and you are encouraged to not just print them out but to edit, add, and tweak in ways that will make each tool most useful to you. Some tools are one-of-a-kind, such as the graphic for "Find Your 20 Percent." Others are variations on the same general idea, so where options exist—as with templates for lesson plans—several are included here.

Now, as for what is not here. Dozens of authors and training practitioners were invited to contribute to this book and were specifically asked for tools they are using in their own work. I thought I had a pretty good idea of what to expect in terms of submissions, and was somewhat surprised at what did not arrive. For instance, no one—not one person—submitted anything on determining training return on investment (ROI). As this is such a hot topic in training-related magazines and books, I don't know whether the lack of submissions is coincidental, that no one had ever needed to create a "homegrown" tool for this, or whether it's a reflection on what is really happening in the field versus what the training literature would have us believe. I have gone back and added some material where reviewers felt its absence would be especially noticed, but let me say again: We asked people to share what they *used*.

Every effort has been made to track down original sources and verify originality. But it's no secret that trainers are "borrowers." For instance, needs assessment instruments, rather like recipes for chocolate pie, all look a bit alike but can be hard to trace to the original authors. Contributors have been very forthcoming about the sources of their material, including the extent to which it has been altered and how much has been reconstructed from faint memory. Please contact me at www.bozarthzone.com if you feel something has not been properly credited, and I'll work to make it right on the website and in future editions of this book. And if you think you have a recipe for a better chocolate pie, well, then, please send that, too.

Jane Bozarth
Durham, North Carolina
October 2007

INTRODUCTION

Purpose

This book grew out of a quest to find real tools and techniques being used in the real world by real training practitioners. While you will likely recognize some of the names here, such as Jean Barbazette, Lou Russell, Patti Shank, Karl Kapp, Jennifer Hofmann, and Saul Carliner, others will be new to you. Many of the items were created by practitioners in need of a solution they couldn't find anywhere else, hence the inclusion of gold-mine material like Colette Haycraft's "Trainer's Planner for Offsite Training," the NC Training Network Team's "Find Your 20 Percent," and Nina Coil's "Seven Principles of Facilitation." Along the way many contributors had other comments, ideas, lessons learned, and "words to the wise" they wanted to share. These have been compiled into lists of quick tips such as "Tips for Working with Subject-Matter Experts" and "Things They Don't Tell You in Train-the-Trainer Courses." Occasionally, an especially relevant anecdote, such as "The Sacred Story vs. The REAL Story," is included as well. Contributors are trainers and facilitators from across industries and continents, such as Delaware, USA, state government, the Genentec biotechnology firm, a Midwestern U.S. casino's training department, and the ZHABA facilitator's collective of Czechoslovakia. One thing the contributors have in common: They are dedicated training professionals willing to share their experiences and solutions.

How This Book Is Organized

In envisioning the approach to this project, intended to be a contributor-provided compilation of materials from the field, acquisitions editor Martin Delahoussaye said, "We need an organizing framework, and ADDIE (Analyze-Design-Develop-Implement-Evaluate) seems to be the model of instructional design that has stuck." Items in this book are therefore fitted into the phases of the ADDIE model (see Table I.1,

1

adapted from a contribution by Jerry Linnins), although at times, when figuring out just where to put things, the lines between ADDIE phases seemed rather blurry (for instance, the templates for storyboarding an e-learning program are used in both the design and develop phases). To help with finding material within chapters, items have been sub-grouped: for instance, in "Chapter 1. Analyze," items addressing learners are grouped separately from those concerned with jobs and tasks.

Table I.1. The ADDIE Process

Phase	Definition	Typical Deliverables	What's Here
ANALYZE	The process of identifying, defining and documenting the need for training or learning intervention to improve performance	Needs Analysis, Job Analysis, Task Analysis, Content Analysis, Learner Analysis, Analysis Report	Templates for collecting data and assessing needs; assessing learner characteristics and technology skills; job and task analysis tools; matrix for documenting existing training— **PLUS** templates for synthesizing and reporting analysis data; tips for gaining management commitment
DESIGN	Based on the identified need(s), the process of creating learning objectives, tests or performance assessments to demonstrate mastery of those objectives, and an overall instructional plan for preparing individuals for passing the tests/mastering the learning objectives	Blueprint of the intervention: list of learning objectives or outcomes; testing plan or performance assessment plan; general structure of the intervention; sequence of material; e-learning outline storyboards	Guidelines for writing objectives; information on creating test items; lesson plan templates; e-learning storyboard templates— **PLUS** tips for good course design; choosing delivery methods; a graphic for finding the critical 20 percent, and design time estimators; tips for working with subject-matter experts (SMEs)

Phase	Definition	Typical Deliverables	What's Here
DEVELOP	Guided by the learning objectives and tests, "develop" is the process of creating appropriate training materials and courseware to support the desired outcomes.	Training visuals; participant materials; instructor guides; learner materials; job aids; e-learning detailed storyboards (for use by programmer)	Guidelines for choosing strategies and instructional methods, such as case studies; templates for lesson plans, syllabi, and facilitator guides; matching activities to learning styles and preferences; tips for developing online programs; guidelines for developing handouts and evaluating visuals. **PLUS** post-design checklists; tips for matching methods to learning styles
IMPLEMENT	The process of piloting and then delivering the designed training/ learning event	Instructor preparation; pilot of training; formative evaluation; regular delivery of training	Tips for managing training, from room logistics to dealing with challenging behaviors; guidelines for giving instructions; instructions for mapping discussion flow—**PLUS** tips for the "lone ranger" trainer; instructor skills assessment form, contents of the traveling trainer's toolkit, ideas for marketing training programs; suggestions for sustaining energy and managing trainer stress; best books for trainers
EVALUATE	The process, ongoing throughout all the phases, of ensuring the need, training design, courseware, and delivery methods are aligned	Kirkpatrick's Four-Level Taxonomy: reaction, learning, application, results/ROI; Stufflebeam CIPP Model: context, input, process, product, sustainability, effectiveness, transferability	Participant reaction form templates; post-mortem checklists for client and team; facilitator assessment of workshop, strategies for assessing at five levels— **PLUS** Formative evaluation tools; overview of the Kirkpatrick and CIPP approaches to evaluation; trainers' evaluation of session

Utilizing ADDIE

A criticism of ADDIE as an approach to design is its linearity and consequent consumption of time. In my work experience, that is often the fault of the individual, not ADDIE itself. It is hard, after all, to argue with the logic of a model for developing training that asks you to assess needs—create the training—conduct the training—evaluate the training. But I have seen developers so caught up in the process and the steps that they never move on to actually getting the thing done. It is possible to analyze a problem until it has gone away (or the employees have retired), and to spend so much time crafting and word-smithing objectives as to completely lose sight of what the training is really intended to accomplish. (I am also thinking at the moment of a colleague who is presently on year *three* of developing a short program on basic skills for new front-line supervisors.) The traditional method of spending months on design, then embarking on a lengthy pilot phase, followed by long periods of revision, does seem cumbersome and antiquated. And: trainers and developers do not operate on limitless funds and open-ended timetables. Management wants a solution, often "yesterday."

There are a number of ways to speed up the ADDIE process, described in training literature as "rapid prototyping" or "rapid design," that speaks to that blurriness I sometimes found in deciding where to place items in the book. The rapid design model views the ADDIE process as less a linear process of distinctive phases (see Figure I.1), and more an endeavor with overlapping phases, as shown in Figure I.2.

Experienced trainers and developers know that training design rarely begins with an utterly blank canvas. For instance, we know that a "stress management" workshop will include at least some mention of relaxation techniques: There's no need to wait until after the needs assessment phase has ended to start casting about for ideas.

Figure I.1. Traditional View of ADDIE

Figure I.2. Rapid Model of ADDIE

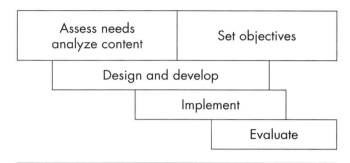

Source: Adapted from Tripp, S., & Bichelmeyer, B. (1990). Rapid prototyping: An alternative instructional design strategy. *Educational Technology Research & Development, 38* (1), 31–44.

Still others—and I am among them—tend to see the instructional design process as iterative and recursive, with phases looping back onto one another. Some ways of speeding up design while maintaining quality:

- Involve the end users up-front. That is, consult with learners at the beginning of the assessment process; don't wait until the program is through the design phase to "pilot." Pilot as you go.

- Do not reinvent the wheel. Find existing survey data and lesson plans on similar topics. Repurpose existing materials, PowerPoint shows, handouts, graphics, and video clips.

- Do technology checks as you go.

- Watch out for project timewasters like team charters, excessive paperwork and reporting requirements, and over-scheduling of standing meetings.

- Leverage technology to save time. Focus group meetings held via virtual meeting formats take far less time than conducting face-to-face sessions, and will likely result in you obtaining better information.

- Fight to have the right people involved, or at least to have the wrong people *un*involved. Too many assessments are skewed, and project teams harmed, by the presence of team members who are only there because of their political connections, place in the organization, and/or ego needs.

- Use ongoing formative evaluation throughout the process rather than wait and do an "evaluation by autopsy" after the training has been completed.

So the further-revised model might look something like the one shown in Figure I.3:

Figure I.3. View of ADDIE as an Iterative, Recursive Process

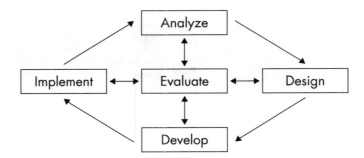

A final criticism of the ADDIE model is that it attempts to make science out of an art. I am inclined to agree. It is nigh impossible to pin down and quantify the elements that make for life-changing training, a-ha moments, and fabulously effective facilitators. This book, though, is written by those who have tried their best to capture those elusive things, who have found perhaps one small solution to one small bedeviling problem, and were willing to share it. Their tools are included on the CD and are meant to be edited to suit your needs. Although assembled in chapters structured around ADDIE, this is a cookbook for busy practitioners, both experienced and novice. Please use the tools here to enhance and extend your own practice and to help move the training profession to the art form it deserves to be.

About the CD

Items that might be best described as "tools," such as templates, checklists, and worksheets, are included on the CD as printable, editable documents. Where a completed sample is provided in the book, a blank version of the tool appears on the CD. Images that are meant as job aids, such as the "ADDIE Wheel" image in Tool 1, are also included as printable objects.

Tool 1. ADDIE Wheel

To get us started, here's a tool from Genentech's Jerry Linnins. A quick but comprehensive overview of ADDIE, it can prove very useful in approaching a new training project in an intentional, planned way, and can help to ensure that steps are not overlooked. I have also found it helpful in explaining the training design process to managers and others requesting design of training.

From Analysis to Evaluation: Tools, Tips, and Techniques for Trainers.
Copyright © 2008 by John Wiley & Sons, Inc. Reproduced by permission of Pfeiffer, an Imprint of Wiley. www.pfeiffer.com

Analyze

The analysis phase is our first chance to "get it right," where we diagnose problems and differentiate training from non-training issues. Experienced practitioners know that, in the "real world," analysis doesn't always (or ever?) occur the way it does in the textbooks. You may be asked to respond to a red-hot urgent request from a CEO, who has little patience for a lengthy analysis phase. You may be called in mid-stream to work from existing data just uncovered in a unit 360-assessment process, or come face-to-face with a manager who has already promised staff a "time management" workshop.

The tools in this chapter are meant to help you find the right solution to the right problem, whether you're working from a quick conversation with a manager or on a full-blown assessment of job and skills tasks. There are worksheets for walking through information with management, templates for conducting task and learner analysis, guidelines for reporting analysis data, and tips for gaining management commitment to proposed training solutions. In addition 'to the usual questions about the symptoms and dysfunctions that point to a need for training, several items invite consideration of end results: What does success look like? As Nanette Miner asks in her "Twenty Questions . . ." list, "How will we know when the problem has gone away?"

Data Collection

When approaching a needs analysis, the training practitioner wears the hat of "researcher," and even "detective." While it is tempting to work only from information provided by managers, within an organization there are many other places for obtaining helpful data. A good analysis typically includes multiple sources of data from different points of view.

Tool 2. Data-Gathering Strategies

Contributed by Thomas Reeves, Ph.D.

This tool offers some suggestions for planning from whom, and how, information can be obtained.

Type of Information	Sources of Information		
	Observations	**Interview**	**Documentation**
Learners	Observe in work environment	Interview target audience, supervisors, peers, customers	Review employee files, training records, or personnel records
Tasks (actual skills used, i.e., data entry, factory assembly)	Observe audience or expert performing	Interview expert or other performers	Review job descriptions, policy statements, and trouble reports
Content (Subject-matter areas, such as "ethics")	Observe expert or creators of product/process	Interview subject-matter experts, policymakers, marketers, or managers	Review product plans, specifications, and marketing guidelines
Organization	Observe groups at work, during training, or company special events; sit in on management meetings	Interview customers, vendors, former employees; format as a "SWOT" analysis of strengths, weaknesses, opportunities, and threats	Company website, marketing materials, annual reports, employee satisfaction surveys, employee exit surveys, HR records, such as grievances and lawsuits

What's the Problem?

It can be awfully tricky getting to the root of the real problem. What the manager describes as a training problem may well be, for instance, a motivation issue that training will not solve: Delivering a group "team-building" workshop will not resolve the problem of the bad egg hired onto the team. Trainers, in their desire to help and to seem responsive, are often guilty of falling into the role of "order taker," as in, "Yes, Mr. Manager! You want an order of Communication Skills with a side of Stress Management!" even though we know the program won't help resolve the concern. As practitioners it's vital to remember that we are here to help managers solve a performance problem, not just deliver a workshop that doesn't address the real issues involved.

The tools in this section were developed by practitioners in need of help in teasing out core issues underlying the presenting symptoms of a problem. As management often sees training as a "quick fix," even if it is not indicated and will not be effective, the tools can be especially helpful in leading managers to consider other, possibly better, solutions. Items are organized from simple/short to complex/detailed. I recommend using the tools in order and as needed; that is, try by beginning with Tool 3. Grid: Is It a Training Problem, where you may find that resolution to the problem will not include a training intervention. Other times you may need to move all the way through to the long, detailed form in Tool 6. Needs substitute Analysis for Training Courses. What you choose, though, depends on your skill, experience, the situation you face, and even your preferences. For instance, I tend to prefer assessments that involve narrative responses and interviews rather than numerical ratings or checklists. Likewise, the tool I use with a client I know well, or a work group I've been with before, is different than one I might choose when first talking with a new client.

Tool 3. Grid: Is It a Training Problem?

I don't know where I first saw this, but there are many slightly different versions out there. I do know that I first discovered it back in the early days of my career and have used it ever since. It's my favorite quick-and-dirty needs assessment tool and has an excellent added value: It is the best tool I know of for helping to communicate the appropriate use of training to a manager making a request. A tip: Go for the "cocktail napkin" effect. I've found managers are even more receptive if you sketch it out while you're talking—as if it's impromptu—than if you pull it out of a file as a preprinted document. This is an excellent, quick tool for separating training issues from other problems.

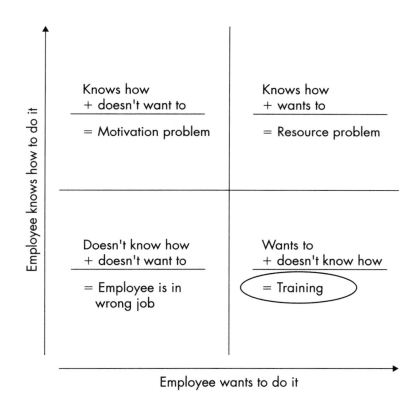

I have found this tool especially useful in talking with a manager who wants to send a seasoned employee to "refresher" training. A training solution is only appropriate for an individual who wants to perform but doesn't know how. If an experienced, previously successful employee— or an entire work unit—suddenly shows a drop-off in performance, then the odds are that the cause lies elsewhere. It could be a motivation problem: Did the company eliminate cash bonuses last quarter? Is the company in the midst of layoffs? Is the individual burning out? Is there trouble at home? If the employee *knows how* to do the job, but *doesn't want to,* you may be looking at a motivation or personal problem.

Is there a resource problem? Does the employee have what he or she needs to perform effectively? I recall a dreadfully frustrating morning when, while trying to set up for a class, the presentation equipment I was using went down beyond repair, the only person with the code to the color copier had simply disappeared, and someone had decided to put a lock on the office supply cabinet without letting the rest of the staff know how to gain access to it. I knew how to do the job, and I wanted to do the job, but endless resource issues kept getting in my way. If the employee *knows how, but can't,* then there may be a resource issue: something is blocking good performance. "Resource" here can mean obstacles ranging from lack of money to broken equipment—even to a weak supervisor.

Has management simply put the wrong person into the job? The occasional bad hire is a universal problem. (Think back to your experiences as a child in school. I'd bet that you had at least one teacher who hated children and performed accordingly.) "Training" won't do anything for the employee who *doesn't know how* to do a job and really *doesn't want to.* Again: If the employee *wants* to do the job, but *doesn't know how,* then training may likely be the right solution. Other conditions would suggest a different response.

Training Manager Susan Nunn offers a comment that recaps the basic issues addressed in the grid: "Trainers are often expected to solve every personnel problem that the manager cannot or does not want to address, so know the difference between a training issue and a performance issue. If the employee *can't* do it, it may well be a training issue. If the employee *won't* do it, it is more likely a management issue. If the *manager* doesn't deal with it, then it may be that it is the manager who needs training to learn to deal with the issue!"

Tool 4. Training Assistance Request Worksheet

Contributed by Linda Levine

A special challenge for training practitioners is conveying the appropriate understanding of training and facilitating an honest assessment of likely outcomes. This form, designed for use in conversations with managers, can help to clarify requests, illuminate problems, and pin down specifics. It would be especially effective used in conjunction with Tool 3. "Grid: Is It A Training Problem?"

1. What do you want your employee(s) to do more, better, differently?

2. What are they currently doing/not doing?

3. What is the effect on the workgroup/customer/ organization?

4. Why do you believe training will resolve the problem?

5. How soon would you like the training offered?

6. How many employees will be participating?

7. Do you have special scheduling requests?

   - Days?
   - Times?

   - Length of Session?
   - Number of Sessions?

Tool 5. Twenty Questions You Should Always Ask Before Starting Any Training Program

Contributed by Nanette Miner, Ed.D.

Here is a longer assessment tool useful for working with managers asking for a particular training solution. It supports a more in-depth examination of a problem and the manager's expectations than the earlier tools. This one also addresses some issues that may surface—such as learner resistance—in delivering the training solution. Creator Nanette Miner, Ed.D,. offers this checklist as the appropriate response to the manager who calls to say, "My team needs sales techniques training."

1. What is the problem you are experiencing?

2. What are the symptoms that led you to believe this was a problem?

3. Who are the learners?

4. Where are the learners?

5. Tell me about their typical day.

6. Why do you think this is a training need?

7. Have they ever been able to do it in the past?

8. What organizational factors might be playing a role?

9. What training exists already?

10. What training have the learners had in the past?

11. Do the learners think they need training? (Now? For this problem?)

12. What if you don't train them? What's the worst that will happen?

13. How will this training need tie to business goals?

14. What's most important to you (the manager): time, speed, or money?

15. What resources are available to assist with this?

16. Who will give their signoff/blessing?

17. How much access will I have to the subject-matter expert?

18. What's the life expectancy of this course?

19. How will the training be reinforced after it's over?

20. How will you know when the problem has gone away? What do you want to see change/done differently?

Tool 6. Needs Analysis for Training Courses

Contributed by Friesen, Kaye and Associates; adapted by Susan Boyd

The preceding tools assume a fairly straightforward request from a manager (or other client) wanting to address an issue with his or her work unit. You may, however, be faced with a problem of farther-reaching scope or one that involves a broader array of organization stakeholders, or you find that you are not comfortable with the amount of information garnered via the other tools. Here is a very comprehensive, detailed needs assessment checklist originally developed by consulting firm Friesen, Kaye and Associates and revised by consultant Susan Boyd. It can aid in problem definition as well as help you find out more about the situation of learners, the constraints in gathering data from other stakeholders, the role of other departments (such as the organization's Information Technology office), and the logistics of the rollout of the training solution.

Category	Question	Response
Business Objectives	1. What business or performance problems are you attempting to resolve or improve?	
	2. What is the impact on the business if this problem is not solved? How important is this problem/issue to the bottom line, reputation, compliance/legal requirements, etc?	
	3. How can training contribute to solving this problem?	
	4. What other things, besides training, have to be done to solve this problem?	
	5. How will success of the project be measured?	
	6. Who will be the business sponsor/leader of the training project?	
	7. What is the budget for the training?	
Training Program Parameters	1. What are the objectives of the training program?	

Category	Question	Response
	2. How does this training program relate to business objectives or goals?	
	3. What incentive or motivation will the learners have if they complete the training?	
	4. What incentive or motivation will the managers have if their staff complete the training?	
	5. What tracking is required for training completion (record of completion, learner test scores, learner's progress through the course, etc.)	
	6. Can the current training tracking system handle the required level of tracking? Is a learning management system in place? If not, will one have to be acquired?	
	7. When is the training required—target date for delivery?	
	8. Will everyone complete the training in a full deployment or will training be completed on a "need to know" basis?	
	9. Who will be on the project team, and what roles will they play? (for example, business lead, IT, training designer, subject-matter experts, representative learners, etc.)	
	10. What content currently exists?	
	11. What is the best way to make the training meaningful to the learners? What work-related documents, scenarios, photos, etc. can be used?	
Learner Assessment	1. Are learners geographically dispersed?	
	2. Do learners work at different times (for example, three shifts)?	

Category	Question	Response
	3. Do the learners see the value or need for this training?	
	4. What is the gap between the learners' current and required skill levels?	
	5. What is the attitude of the learners about the topic area?	
	6. What do learners already know about the topic?	
	7. What is the motivation of the learners to complete this training?	
	8. What information is known about the demographics of the learner population (age, gender, education level, etc.)?	
	9. Will the course first be piloted to targeted groups of learners?	
	10. What types of training programs have succeeded with these learners?	
	11. What types of training programs have *not* succeeded with these learners?	
	12. What are the technology skills of the learners?	
	13. What is their acceptance of technology delivered learning?	
	14. What are the cultural and language needs/preferences of the learners?	
	15. Is there support for learning at the desktop from managers and other learners?	
Technology Assessment	1. Is the IT department part of the project team for the training department?	
	2. What equipment setup do the learners have (hardware speed, Internet connection, browser version, sound cards, headsets, etc.)?	

Category	Question	Response
	3. What software plug-ins are already part of the standard configuration? Can others be added?	
	4. What authoring tools can be used (or are in place) to create online learning?	
	5. What provisions are there for learners to take courses at another work station if they do not have a desktop or the needed setup?	
	6. What bandwidth issues should be considered?	
	7. What are the technical requirements for the LMS system, if any?	
Assessment Strategies	1. What is the most effective assessment strategy for your audience (e-mail survey, telephone survey, in-person interview, focus group)?	
	2. What is the availability of staff to participate in assessments, such as interviews or focus groups?	

Tip: Saying, "No."

What if, in the course of conducting a needs assessment, you find that the problem simply does not suggest a training solution? Providing the wrong solution in response to a request is a version of winning the battle but losing the war: The training department gets the business and seems responsive, but, ultimately, someone will say, "Well, we tried training, but it didn't work" or, worse, "The training department did this for us, but it didn't help at all." It is a disservice to the client and a blow to the training profession's credibility. But how to say, "No" to a boss, or even to *your* boss? Remember, managers, even those who are insisting on training, really are asking to have a problem solved. Showing how that can be done, and being part of that better solution, will ultimately enhance both training's and your reputation. While there may be times you simply must follow orders, work to position the training function as a partner in performance improvement, not just the deliverer of one type of intervention.

Job, Task, and Skills Analysis

A thorough needs assessment involves more than just interviews with management. Tools 7, 8, and 9 offer help in analyzing specifics of performance.

Tool 7. Job/Content Analysis

Contributed by Thomas Reeves, Ph.D.

If your program is intended to train people for a specific job or task, such as training a procurement officer to use a new spreadsheet function, you will usually conduct a "job analysis." If your program is aimed at educating people about a specific content or subject area, such as "workplace ethics," you will usually conduct a "content analysis." Both types of analysis are quite similar, and in most cases, your analysis will include both job and content analysis.

JOB ANALYSIS			
Job Title: Description of the Job:			
Tasks	**Tools Used**	**Standards for Performance**	**Conditions for Performance**

CONTENT ANALYSIS			
Subject Area Title: Content Description and Relevant Definitions:			
Tasks	**Tools Used**	**Standards for Performance**	**Conditions for Performance**

Tool 8. Task Analysis Form

Here is a tool for a more in-depth task analysis. The prospect of task analysis can be daunting, but can be critical to successful problem diagnosis and subsequent solution. The tools below provide a nuts-and-bolts overview of ways to approach the process. Breaking a task down, though, can be quite an undertaking. Take a look, if you can, at Designing Effective Instruction *by Morrison, Ross, and Kemp (3rd ed. 2001). It includes a task analysis for making a peanut butter and jelly sandwich—all sixty-eight steps.*

Task Analysis Form: Outline

1. Identify the major user tasks and criticality of each.

2. Break tasks down into subtasks and specific steps.

3. Identify frequency and priority of each step or subtask.

4. Identify input and display requirements.

Below is part of a sample task analysis using an outline format.

I. Major Task 1: Create an order (Criticality: Critical; Frequency: order rate 50/hour)

   A. Subtask 1: Enter customer data (system will generate and display order number)

      a. Step 1.1. Enter last name: 100 percent of time

      b. Step 1.2. Enter first name: 100 percent of time

      c. Step 1.3. Enter phone number: 90 percent of time (customer does not always have phone)

   B. Subtask 2: Enter order information

      a. Step 2.1. Enter item number: 100 percent of time, required

      b. Step 2.2. Enter quantity: 95 percent of time only 1; 5 percent of time quantity is more than 1

      c. Step 2.3. Enter color: 25 percent of time this field is used

If you prefer, the task analysis data can be entered in table form, as shown in the sample below.

Task Analysis Form: Table					
Task	**Description of Task or Step**	**Frequency**	**Data to Be Displayed**	**Input Fields**	**Criticality of Task**
Major Task 1	Create an order	*50 hour*			Critical
Subtask A.1.	Enter customer data	Always	*Order number assigned by system*	*Last name, first name, phone, address*	
Step A.1.1	Enter last name	*Always*			
Step A.1.2	Enter first name	*Always*			
Step A.1.3	Enter phone#	*90 percent of time*			

Source: NASA

Tool 9. Skills Chart

Contributed by Karl Kapp, Ph.D.

From contributor Karl Kapp: "Often there is a disconnect between what an organization says is important and where the organization decides to focus its training resources. This skills chart is designed to determine the gap between the skills that the organization views as critical to success and the perception of how successful training is for building those skills. During the needs analysis process, a tool like this can expose gaps between critical organizational skills and training that may be needed.

Getting training resources can be a difficult task; however, demonstrating a clear gap between the critical skills an organization needs for success and the effectiveness of the training programs to address those skills can be a real eye opener for management. It really highlights the difference between lip service about critical skills and actions taken to strengthen those skills. Also, if management and hourly employees differ on what skills are critical or what training is effective, that difference can open up a dialogue within the organization to address those gaps."

How to Use the Skills Chart

The Skills Chart in Tool 9 should be used at the organizational level with both management and hourly employees to determine, overall, the critical skills within the organization and how effective the training efforts are in helping employees achieve those skills. When you have gathered all the input from the employees, add up the numbers on the scale and create a weighted average. You may find that a certain skill is Extremely Critical to your organization but that the training is Not Effective. You may also find that management deems one skill Extremely Critical, while hourly employees may deem a different skill as Extremely Critical. Creating a graph juxtaposing critical skills and the effectiveness of training can really highlight training gaps.

How to Customize the Skills Chart

To customize this chart, list the general skills you think are important to your organization, especially those that have surfaced during your analysis. The example shown deals with a transportation company. If you worked in a manufacturing company, you might indicate skills like grinding, lathe operation, and so forth. If you worked with a banking company, you might pick skills like customer relations, cross-selling, or other related items. You may have to conduct focus groups to create the initial list of skills. Once you have the list narrowed down, place the skills on the skills chart and seek input from the organization. You do not need to have specific names, but it is a good idea to determine position within the organization to identify any gaps that may exist between management and hourly employees.

Training Needs Analysis: Skills Chart

Type of Skills	1 = Extremely Critical 5 = Not Critical How critical are the following skills to your organization?	1 = Extremely Effective 5 = Not Effective How effective is the training your employees are currently receiving in this area?	Internal or External Is the training conducted internally or externally? If externally, please indicate provider.
Mechanics			
Diesel Engine Repair	1 2 3 4 5	1 2 3 4 5 (no training)	Int/Ext Provider:
Truck Body Repair	1 2 3 4 5	1 2 3 4 5 (no training)	Int/Ext Provider:
Trailer Repair	1 2 3 4 5	1 2 3 4 5 (no training)	Int/Ext Provider:
Preventative Maintenance/Mechanics	1 2 3 4 5	1 2 3 4 5 (no training)	Int/Ext Provider:
Organization/Time Management	1 2 3 4 5	1 2 3 4 5 (no training)	Int/Ext Provider:
Drivers			
Understanding life as a driver	1 2 3 4 5	1 2 3 4 5 (no training)	Int/Ext Provider:
Customer Service	1 2 3 4 5	1 2 3 4 5 (no training)	Int/Ext Provider:
Interpersonal Skills	1 2 3 4 5	1 2 3 4 5 (no training)	Int/Ext Provider:
Driver-Specific Paperwork (understanding importance, DOT requirements)	1 2 3 4 5	1 2 3 4 5 (no training)	Int/Ext Provider:
Computer Skills	1 2 3 4 5	1 2 3 4 5 (no training)	Int/Ext Provider:
General Workforce			
English as a second language (Spanish) or Other (specify)	1 2 3 4 5	1 2 3 4 5 (no training)	Int/Ext Provider:
Diversity Training	1 2 3 4 5	1 2 3 4 5 (no training)	Int/Ext Provider:
Computer Skills	1 2 3 4 5	1 2 3 4 5 (no training)	Int/Ext Provider:
Written and Oral, Communication Skills	1 2 3 4 5	1 2 3 4 5 (no training)	Int/Ext Provider:
Team-Building Skills, Interpersonal Skills	1 2 3 4 5	1 2 3 4 5 (no training)	Int/Ext Provider:

Analysis: Learners

Another activity important to a strong analysis is garnering knowledge about the target audience. It is critical that training design address not just organizational needs but the attitudes, abilities, and realities of those who will receive the training. Several of the tools provided have already touched on issues of learner attitude toward training and past training experiences. Tool 10 is an in-depth questionnaire for use in gathering data about a target training group as a whole. Creator Karl Kapp uses it to paint a portrait of a sample learner group, representing the population for whom training will be developed. I know of one organization, with a training department offering a large catalog of courses for which employees can enroll themselves (such as Excel and Stress Management and Negotiation Skills), that collects this data from every new hire. The information is stored in a database and then, prior to a class, the training department can pull up a composite picture of the attendees. The trainer can then better plan activities and anticipate needs and questions.

As so many organizations are now moving to e-learning approaches, a technology skills inventory (Tool 11) is also included in this section. Both of these items touch on information regarding the learning styles of individual learners.

A final note on the matter of learning styles and preferences: There are myriad theories on learning styles. The most prominent are perhaps those based on Kolb's Cycle of Learning and Gardner's Theory of Multiple Intelligences. Information regarding these and other theories is largely previously published and copyrighted but is widely available on the Internet; try a web search for "learning styles." The underlying assumption for any of the theories is, briefly, that all learners have particular styles and preferences in how they learn, and therefore the conscientious trainer will prepare materials and approaches that address all preferences (for instance, a mix of written work, presentation, and hands-on activities). A quick test can be pulled from the Visual-Auditory-Kinesthetic (VAK) model, which asks whether a learner prefers to learn via seeing, hearing, or touching. Here's an example: When you buy a new piece of electronic equipment—a new cell phone, say—do you sit down and read through the entire manual, talk with a friend who has a similar phone, or just play with it until it works? The first indicates a visual learning preference, the second an auditory preference, and the third, a kinesthetic preference. Knowing the mix of styles in your group of learners, particularly if it is heavily skewed toward or away from a particular preference (for instance, a strong preference for hands-on activities and an aversion to written material and reading assignments), will be helpful in planning an effective training intervention.

Tool 10. Learner Characteristics

Contributed by Karl Kapp, Ph.D.

This tool helps to paint a portrait of a sample audience, representative of the target population for whom the training will be developed. A filled-in example is shown.

Example: Acme Tool & Die, Third Shift, October 2007

Learner Characteristics	Data Collected	Resources Used
Age	Age Ranges 20–25	Self-Report
Gender	Six male, two female	Self-Report
Language	Primarily English as a first language; One: First language Indian; Two: First language Spanish	Self-Report
Work Experience	As most are under age 25, this is first full-time job	Self-Report
Position Within Organization	Front-line assembly staff	Organizational chart
Personal Characteristics		
Maturity level	Most are young and there are occasional problems with impulse control and work habits	Floor supervisor
Motivation Level	Overall high; two employees have expressed interest in moving up; one is working third shift in order to attend college during the day	Floor supervisor
Expectations	Frequent pay increases; comfortable work environment with added perks: espresso machine, massage chairs in break room	Floor supervisor; self-report
Vocational aspirations	Some interested in upward movement; one moving to engineering upon completion of degree; others seem satisfied	Self-Report
Special Talents/interests	Two very interested in virtual worlds and are Second Life participants, one a voracious reader, one a sci-fi movie fancier; one especially interested in factory floor operations; one especially good with troubleshooting machinery glitches	Self-Report
Mechanical dexterity	Very high: job demands it	Observation of learners

Learner Characteristics	Data Collected	Resources Used
Ability to work under various environmental conditions	Has not been assessed; factory floor does not change	N/A
Academic Information		
Education completed	High school; six with one year of college; one with two years of college; one college graduate	HR records
Training level completed	All have had intro courses; two have had advanced troubleshooting; one in beginning supervisory skills training	Training record review
Special courses completed	One has attended high-level safety training and serves as shift safety manager/consultant	Training record review
Previous performance levels	Satisfactory; one seems to become bored with mundane nature of work, resulting in slightly higher rate of rework	Floor supervisor
Standardized test scores	N/A	N/A
GPA	N/A	N/A
Learning Styles		
Visual/Auditory /Kinesthetic preference	Perception of Information: Visual, Auditory, Kinesthetic. Primarily Kinesthetic	Observation of learners; learner responses to web quiz: "How Do you Learn Best?"

Tool 11. Learner Technology Skills

Contributed by Karl Kapp, Ph.D.

In my experience, asking only management about employee technology skills doesn't help me find very good information. For instance, I was once told that the employees of an accounting unit were proficient only in spreadsheet and other numbers-based applications, but in talking with employees found that several spent their lunch hour participating in a complex role-playing online game, while another had taught herself web design and was creating a family genealogy website. Contributor Karl Kapp had similar experiences and developed this questionnaire in advance of implementation of a new enterprise-wide software system. It would be useful for any organization planning a technology rollout or launching e-learning to a new learner group. The data collected here could prove invaluable in smoothing a launch, anticipating user skill issues, and creating prework activities. Several questions in the "learning styles" section would be useful in any assessment of learners.

PC Skills

1. What do you use a computer for at work?

   ❑ Email

   ❑ Web/information searches

   ❑ Spreadsheets (Excel or others)

   ❑ Documentation (Word)

   ❑ Presentations (PowerPoint)

   ❑ Work processes (ordering, tracking, etc)

   ❑ Other use (instant messaging, gaming, other)

2. How proficient do you feel that you are in the different software you use?

3. Do you use a computer at home? If yes, what for?

   ❑ Financial tracking/budgets?

   ❑ Web (if web, what do you use the web for?)

❑   Information

❑   Travel planning

❑   Pay bills

❑   Games

❑   Email

❑   Other

Learning Styles

1. How did you learn to use the computer software that you currently use?

2. How do you feel that you learn best? (classroom instruction, reading on your own, experience)

3. If you could obtain additional training, coaching, or support on any software that you use, which applications would you want support/ training on? Why?

4. What would the best type of training/support for you look like?

❑   Formal class

❑   Coaching

❑   Book

❑   Tech support online

❑   Other

5. Of the software training that you have attended,

   - What parts did you feel were the most beneficial?

   - What parts were the most frustrating for you?

6. If you currently have a question about how to use software, whom do you ask?

7. Do you have any software manuals you use to find information?

8. What is the best training experience you have ever had? What made it good?

9. What is the worst training experience you have ever had? What made it bad?

Tool 12. Existing Training: Who Gets What?

Still another element of needs assessment is finding out what is already in place and what learners have experienced or been exposed to. This can help the person conducting the analysis to understand what training learners have already attended and what types of training the organization supports, and it can shed light on the learners' experience with training in this particular workplace. This matrix is also useful at communicating training requirements and is a good item to provide to new hires and supervisors.

Course	Jobs Requiring Training	Duration	Frequency
A/C Refrigeration Servicing	A/C Maintenance	5 hours	New hire
HAZWOPPER First responder	Security	8 hours	Annual
Environmental Awareness	Bulk Materials; Integrated Emergency Response; Spill Contingency; Waste Management; Energy Management; Asbestos Management	6 hours	Every other year
Incident Command	Security and Supervisors	12 hours	Annual
Fire Brigade	Emergency Response Team	2 hours	New hire
EMS Awareness	All staff and full-time on-site contractors		New hire and as necessary
EMS Document	Staff and full-time on-site contractors whose work requires knowledge of the document	Varies	New hire and when document changes occur
EMS Implementation	Cross-Functional Team and EMR	8 hours	New hire and new auditors

Source: North Carolina Division of Pollution Prevention and Environmental Assistance

Synthesizing and Reporting Data

What to do with all the data once it is gathered? Here are two tools useful in synthesizing and making sense of the information culled during the analysis phase. The first, Tool 13, is for use by the trainer or other person conducting the analysis, to help in sorting out different sources and points of view. Tool 14 is a suggested format for crafting the analysis report form that will be submitted to management or other client.

Tool 13. Training Analysis Recap for Trainer

Once analysis is complete, this tool is helpful in organizing and recapping the data and reducing it to its essence. As the tool emphasizes the perspectives of different stakeholders, it can be useful in identifying and analyzing situations that may involve "touchy" subject matter or political issues. The last steps ask for a preliminary description of both short-term and long-term solutions as well as an analysis of possible outcomes if the solution is implemented. I find this tool very helpful in assembling data from various sources into a meaningful whole.

Regarding the source of this item: Several years ago, in a graduate school class, we used a document similar to this in analyzing cases from the textbook. The professor has since moved on and the book is out of print. Much later, in the course of working on a project, I felt the need to use the worksheet again, reconstructed it as best I remembered it, and have modified it since. Here is a completed form showing an example, including my shorthand and notes to myself, of a real case I encountered.

Needs Analysis Recap

Project: *Government agency request for online "discipline policy" training*

1. **Summarize: What are the critical facts, key information, key players, resources, and constraints? (Note: Avoid jumping to "solutions" at this point.)**

Management request: develop an online program for the state's employee discipline process.

Main issues: Grievances are increasing and being lost in bigger ways. Losses are typically due to serious errors, such as blatant discrimination, and not to mistakes with finer points of the policy. Prior training has been provided by subject-matter experts in HR offices and is reportedly dry, too technical and intricate, and too focused on rules and procedures than on application.

2. **What are the main issues? What is at the heart of this situation?**

Grievances are not lost due to small policy matters such as sending the wrong memo or failing to follow every item on the policy to a "t." They are revealing serious issues with failure to help employees improve, inconsistency in treatment of employees across the work unit, and blatant cases of discrimination and favoritism. Supervisors are able to apply the letter of the policy, but are missing the intent.

3. What are the different perspectives of those involved?

Upper management is concerned about costs and bad publicity associated with lost cases and acknowledges that existing training is not working. Very supportive of alternative training delivery methods as traditional classroom has proven time-consuming, expensive, and difficult to schedule so that supervisors can attend. Specifically requested and offered support for online training program.

Middle management thinks that the policies are too intricate and that training offered has been only in the form of presenting detail about policy, not application to realistic situations. Learner reaction sheets consistently report that materials used in training do not reflect reality of workplace situations and constraints on supervisors.

There is stress between management and the human resources offices: Management feels that the HR offices are not providing enough support and meaningful information about effective use of the policies.

Agency in-house subject-matter experts (HR staff) reluctantly provide training, but have no experience with instructional design and thus regard training only as presentation of material.

Learners say they have little input into the process or the content of training provided to them, feel that the training content is overwhelming, too focused on details and facts rather than application, and not relevant to their work realities. Training viewed as a waste of their time.

Additional learner information: As a group learners are in their mid-thirties to mid-forties, college graduates. Have strong word processing and email skills, but have limited experience with e-learning. Learners predominantly have visual/kinesthetic learning preference. They are not auditory and have expressed complaints with lecture-heavy training.

4. What are the known facts?

Grievances are increasing and being lost.

Cases not lost on technicalities but on blatant errors.

Management wants a new training program, preferably online, targeted to reduce the issues that are causing the increased grievances.

Those who developed the existing training are subject-matter experts with heavy focus on content but little on application; current training consists largely of coverage of "rules" and details.

There is a credibility gap between HR specialists and managers/learners.

HR specialists have ownership in the program, are threatened by potential changes and especially the idea that the new program can be delivered online.

5. What do you still need to find out? (Be mindful of time frames.)

Who is making the rules about the "need"? Are there other perspectives? Whose needs are being neglected? WIIFM for learners; what are their real concerns?

A concern: The focus seems entirely on the issue with grievances themselves. But the grievances are caused by underlying issues such as favoritism and discrimination. What do we need to do about that?

What are the critical skills needed by the line managers who must administer the policy? (Need to complete a task analysis). For instance, does the line manager actually write warning letters or conduct disciplinary meetings alone?

6. Ideas for short-term solution? What can you do now that will help satisfy the client?

Quickly create job aids, checklists, and flowcharts of processes/procedures (solutions close to the performance context)—find ways to simplify the complexity of the policy and make procedures more accessible.

Include end users in design.

Find/develop authentic scenarios and case studies for training.

Use extant data (grievances are published, so review these cases) for rapid instructional design.

Involve subject-matter experts in design and deployment.

Need to establish plan for overcoming objections: Approach will mean less coverage of material, nontraditional "look."

"Sell" the advantages of the online learning approach.

Repurpose existing materials.

Develop and deploy the online program.

7. Ideas for a long-term solution?

Work toward culture change.

Develop work for HR staff: Cases are not lost entirely because of supervisors. Upper management and HR must sign off on everything; cases should not be making it past them.

Updates and ongoing performance support

Library of tools

Consistency among agencies

8. Advantages/disadvantages of solutions. (Consider the needs of the different stakeholders.)

Advantages: Problem solved; players satisfied; more meaningful learning used in relevant contexts

Disadvantages: fails; technology fails; training not delivered

9. Anticipated outcomes if client implements recommendations:

Fewer grievances—resolution of presenting problem. Employees receive fairer treatment. Management satisfied. Learners confident at handling. Paves way for future problem-based blended or online programs.

Tool 14: Analysis Report Template

Contributed by Thomas Reeves, Ph.D.

Just as it is important to conduct a good needs assessment, it is also essential to report the findings in a clear, concise manner that decision-makers can understand and use. While the preceding recap form was intended for the trainer to use, the form below is intended for use in developing the information to be presented to management or other clients. The "Analysis Report Template" lists the items that should be included in a needs assessment or task analysis report. The formality of the report will depend on the size and scope of the project and the nature of your relationship with the client.

Executive Summary: This section presents an overview of the analysis findings in a format that allows decision makers to make important decisions effectively and efficiently.

Introduction: This section introduces the major sections of the report as well as the primary people involved in conducting the analysis and producing the report. The client is also clearly identified.

Background: This section describes any information needed to provide the reader with an understanding of the background for the analysis, for example, who initiated it and why.

Purpose(s): This section describes the purpose(s) of the analysis. For example, a needs assessment might be done to detect training or education needs that aren't being met by existing programs. Or a needs assessment might be done to confirm the existence of needs or clarify the nature of needs that others have perceived. A job or task analysis might be undertaken to collect information directly related to the nature of the interactive multimedia product under development.

Limitations: This section spells out any limitations to the interpretation and generalizability of the analysis. It should also describe threats to the reliability and validity of the instruments (e.g., questionnaires, interview protocols, or focus group protocols) used in the analysis.

Questions: This section outlines specific questions asked, and of whom.

Methods: This section describes the analysis techniques used, such as observations and surveys. Step-by-step descriptions of *what was* done should be provided.

Sample: This section describes the managers, learners, trainers, and other personnel included in the analysis.

Instrumentation: This section describes all the instruments and tools that were used during the analysis. Copies of the tools should be included in the Appendices.

Results: This section spells out the findings. Graphs and charts should be used wherever they are appropriate.

Recommendations: This section presents recommendations based on the findings report in the previous section.

Summary: This section presents a brief synopsis of the report.

References: This last section lists the sources reviewed or consulted during the analysis.

Chapter 1 Wrap-Up

Here are some words to the wise offered by experienced practitioners, lessons learned about bridging the analysis phase with the movement to the design phase. This section concludes with Tool 15, the "World's Quickest Training Needs Analysis" worksheet.

Analysis: The REAL Story Versus the Sacred Story

I learned one of my most valuable lessons in needs analysis in a serendipitous "a-ha" moment during a graduate course on Reflective Practice. The professor put a pile of school catalogs, the campus newspaper, and some departmental brochures on the table in front of us and asked us to spend five minutes writing the "story" about our university those materials told.

The glossy marketing materials showed deliriously happy students, and a diverse bunch at that, working in chemistry labs and listening intently to professors and working with what appeared to be very expensive lab equipment and things like nuclear reactors. So our lists were pretty much the same, with lots of phrases like "cutting edge," "technologically advanced," "high-tech," and "research of global importance."

When we'd finished and reviewed our lists out loud, the professor said, "You've just told this university's sacred story. Now look around this room and down the hall, and cast about in your memory, and spend five minutes writing this university's *real* story."

I looked around the room. We, enrolled in doctoral studies in this large, "technologically advanced, cutting-edge" university, were meeting in a classroom that had a *chalk*board (with no chalk), an overhead projector with no bulb, and a leak-stained interior wall. And we were all white. And we were all middle-class.

Moral: In talking with management and other stakeholders about training needs, be aware that you'll likely be given the sacred story. Find the *real* story before you start developing training. It will help you get at the true training issues, it will shore up your credibility with the trainees, it will help you design a more effective evaluation strategy, and it will help you shift the role of trainer from "order taker" to performance consultant.

Tips for Achieving Management Commitment to Training Solutions

Contributed by Patti Shank, Jennifer Hofmann, and Cindy Epps

Getting management commitment to training, to ensure employees are allowed and encouraged to attend, and to support the transfer of training back to the work site, can be quite a challenge. Even when the training is indicated by performance problems, and sometimes even when it has been requested by a manager, freeing up staff time to attend training and supporting participation by staff can still prove something of a struggle. Here are some tips from seasoned trainers and instructional designers. Many, one way or another, speak to the need for training to address the right issues and solve real problems.

- Work toward performance improvement, not just "training," so *real* problems are solved.

- Listen. Don't interrupt. Learn how the organization really works.

- NO mandatory classes. If your instruction isn't good enough for folks to *want* to attend, you aren't doing your job, and managers can only do so much to support you. Even if the courses are mandated by law or something else, there's no need to announce it.

- Have line management involved in the analysis and course development phase so you know what the problems are and what they need. This will also help to gain their support in helping learners transfer new skills back to the work site.

- Set an expectation that line management is primarily responsible for skill development for their staff. They know those jobs better than you do. Your job is to produce the training their folks need. Make it a partnership. Provide a valuable service and real solutions, not just "training."

- Understand the jobs you are developing training for by shadowing staff and managers, doing the jobs, and walking in their shoes.

- Don't get sucked into fads and easy answers.

- Have orientations for managers about new initiatives, emphasizing the "what's in it for you" factor.

- Make managers responsible for signing off that training has occurred. Establish managers as the final assessors.

- Be credible. Don't make promises you can't keep—and keep the ones you make.

- Focus on those things you have control over, such as providing data to managers about performance issues or training needs.

- Make an explicit link between your training and your training marketing materials to the organization's mission, vision, and values.

- Help learners make connections between their performance and the organization's goals.

- Invite managers to present modules in your sessions.

Tool 15. World's Quickest Training Needs Analysis

Contributed by Anne Howard and the founding members of the NC Trainers' Network Team.

Many training practitioners wear several hats, and are often analyzers, designers, trainers, and evaluators all in one. The first key principle, and cornerstone, of the North Carolina Certified Training Specialist course is: "Learner First, Situation Second, Content Third." The tool below is the first item presented to novice trainers attending the course, and they are told again and again: If you don't do anything else, at least do this.

Who Are My Learners?

1. What do most of them do on the job?

2. What do the rest do?

3. Why are they participating in this training?

4. Is it required? If so, by whom?

5. What do they already know about this topic?

6. What reactions/problems do I anticipate?

7. How many people do I expect?

8. Do they have a history with me on this topic? What is that history?

What Is the Situation?

1. How much time do I have for the training session?

2. How many people must be trained at once?

3. How many sessions are needed?

4. Will I have to travel to the training site? Will I have to carry equipment?

5. What size room do I have?

6. Are tables available?

7. Is there room for participants to move around?

8. What resources are available to me? (e.g., co-trainers, pre-designed activities, audiovisual equipment)

9. Are there statutory requirements that must be met? If so, what are they?

What Do They Need to Know?

1. What are the expectations of those requesting the training?

2. What are the expectations of the learners?

3. How do people who use this information or skill use it?

4. What is the crucial 20 percent of content that the learners *must* know when they leave this training?

5. What can they reference following the training?

Additional Suggested Resources

The tools and tips contained here were developed by practitioners working in the trenches in response to a need they felt was not being met by other resources. In practice, their work is supplemented, or perhaps inspired by, material from the training literature and more "famous" names in the field. For instance, an excellent diagnostic tool is Mager and Pipe's needs analysis flow chart, easily found in an Internet search, and there are myriad online resources for information on assorted learning style theories. For a comprehensive resource on the "analysis" phase of ADDIE, try Ron Zemke and Thomas Kramlinger's excellent book *Figuring Things Out* (Reading, MA: Addison Wesley, 1982).

Design

n the design phase we take our knowledge of the need and translate it into measurable performance objectives. This is the blueprinting stage, in which we identify entry behaviors, create the bare-bones outline, draft an instructional plan, and design the tests and other performance measures that will be used to assess whether the instruction has been successful.

In the excitement of moving to the development phase it is tempting to skip or skim activities that will ultimately give better results. Time spent clarifying meaningful objectives, crafting a sound evaluation plan, and developing assessments before creating content will pay off in more effective programs and instructional experiences. L. Dee Fink notes, in Tool 36, the importance of laying a good foundation to ensure development of a good final product.

This chapter includes items useful for blueprinting a training project: worksheets for creating sound objectives, suggestions for developing effective tests, guidelines for choosing among delivery formats, templates for lesson planning and storyboarding, cost and time estimators, and project planning tools.

Tool 16. Find Your 20 Percent

Contributed by the NC Training Network Team

Too often training design begins by amassing all the content that could be covered and then figuring out how to squeeze it into the available time. <u>Good</u> training starts from the "inside out": begin with what learners absolutely must know, then build the instruction outward from there. Find the critical 20 percent of the information—the crucial two or three key points, and add on only what enhances that. This is an especially useful tool for those who struggle with culling the "must know" information from the "nice to know." A good rule of thumb: Training design is done when there's nothing left to take out.

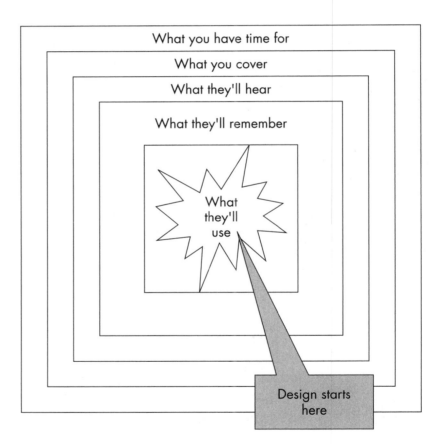

Developing Objectives

Following are a number of tools for developing learning objectives. It is critical to the success of the training initiative to begin with the end in mind: What, specifically, is the desired outcome? As noted in the Introduction, it is possible to get so caught up in wordsmithing as to lose sight of what the training is intended to do. Other times it seems objectives are generated as a perfunctory task, even perhaps as an afterthought. When developing objectives, be sure to stay focused on desired outcomes, and ensure that those outcomes, in turn, focus on real-world performance. For instance, in researching this book I ran across a lesson plan for a workshop called "Instructional Design for Trainers ." One of the objectives was, "The participant will be able list the items that should be included in an instructor manual." Clients hire me to *produce* detailed participant guides, not list the items that should be included in one. A more meaningful, performance-targeted objective would be something like: "You will create an example of a completed instructor manual according to the criteria provided."

This section opens with some tips from "Training Doctor" Nanette Miner, followed by guidelines for, and examples of , objectives, and a worksheet for writing learning objectives.

Tips for Creating Objectives: Rules of Thumb and Common Errors

Contributed by Nanette Miner, Ed.D.

Two Objectives in One

Don't combine two objectives into one, such as: Participant will locate air filter and determine whether it should be replaced. What if your participant can locate the filter but cannot determine whether it should be replaced? Did he pass the objective or fail it?

Knowing and Understanding

Avoid objectives that aim to improve an internal state of mind; for example, to "understand" or to "know" are not measurable or observable. In addition, since most learning in the workplace is to achieve a performance outcome, these two terms truly are inapplicable—there is almost always an action word that describes what your learners will leave knowing or being able to do. (See Tool 17, "Types of Objectives: Seven Levels," for suggestions for action words.)

Too Broad

You don't want your objectives to be so broad that three different instructors, given your objective, could teach three different classes. For example: "Participants will be able to read financial statements."

Stating a Topic as an Objective

Many times a designer will state a topic, such as: "Participants will learn the principles of electricity," rather than a learning objective, which might be stated: "Learners will be able to wire an electric engine." In this case the principles of electricity would be inherent in learning how to wire an electric engine.

Teaching Versus Performance

Similar to stating a topic as an objective, many times objectives are erroneously stated in the form of what is being taught, rather than in the form of what the trainee will be able to *do*. For instance, "reading financial statements" is what is being taught, but "identifying uses of cash reserves" is what you want the learner to be able to do as a result of the training.

Tool 17. Types of Objectives: Seven Levels

I'm guessing that readers involved in training and instructional design have at least a passing knowledge of Benjamin Bloom's taxonomy of objectives, which describes learning in terms of level of sophistication. If you envision Bloom's ideas as a ladder, the lowest level, knowledge, addresses only recall and provides training that asks learners to do little more than recite a series of steps in a process or memorize some definitions of terms. The remaining climb up the ladder would include, in order, comprehension, application, analysis, synthesis, and evaluation. (This is an extremely truncated explanation, meant as a quick reminder for those with a background with Bloom; those unfamiliar with his work are encouraged to perform a web search for "Bloom's taxonomy.") This tool outlines the levels of the taxonomy and offers suggestions for action words—the root of learner performance objectives—appropriate for each, followed by examples of completed objectives.

Action Words for Each Level			
1. Fact Objectives	Define	Name	Record
	List	Repeat	State
	Recall	Recognize	Record
2. Understanding or Comprehension Objectives	Discuss	Describe	Explain
	Identify	Translate	Restate
	Express	Convert	Estimate
3. Application Objectives	Compute	Demonstrate	Illustrate
	Operate	Perform	Interpret
	Apply	Use	Practice
4. Analysis Objectives	Solve	Compare	Appraise
	Distinguish	Contrast	Classify
	Differentiate	Categorize	Critique
5. Synthesis Objectives	Synthesize	Design	Summarize
	Diagnose	Manage	Plan
	Propose	Hypothesize	Formulate
6. Attitudinal Objectives	Show sensitivity	Respect opinions	Be willing to assist
	Accept responsibility	Demonstrate commitment	

7. Skill Objectives	Perform	Demonstrate	Show
	Compute	Teach	Role play
	Operate	Complete	Design
	Conduct	Take	Do

Examples of Objectives	
Fact Objective	*By the end of this training, you will be able to* list four risk factors for skin cancer.
Understanding Objective	*By the end of this training, you will be able to* describe three ways parents can protect their children from the harmful effects of UV radiation.
Application Objective	*By the end of this training, you will be able to* demonstrate your ability to use the Physician Data Query to research information on cancer clinical trials related to two case studies.
Analysis Objective	*By the end of this training, you will be able to* contrast the barriers to fecal occult blood testing and colonoscopy by naming two barriers that are similar and two barriers that are different.
Synthesis Objective	*By the end of this training, you will be able to* design an action plan to increase community awareness of the importance of cancer clinical trials through working within their own community-based organizations.
Attitudinal Objective	*By the end of this training, you will be able to* demonstrate a commitment to increasing the number of women aged fifty or older who get mammograms by agreeing to tell five friends in the next three months to schedule a mammogram.
Skill Objective	*By the end of this training, you will be able to* perform a correct clinical breast exam using the vertical strip method by demonstrating this to the trainer during a simulation exercise with two standardized patients.

Source: National Cancer Institute

Tool 18. Writing Objectives: Worksheet

A complete objective, particularly one that goes beyond the "fact" and "understanding" levels, not only lists who will do what, but provides specifics about performance criteria. This worksheet is helpful in thinking through the elements of a thorough objective.

	Who	What	Under What Conditions	How Well	When	Other
Objective 1	Health Care Technician	Distinguish abnormal heartbeat from normal	Using stethoscope	100 percent of the time	During shift rounds	Alert nurse if abnormality is suspected
Objective 2						
Objective 3						
Objective 4						

Source: National Cancer Institute

Testing

Once objectives are set, the designer must determine how he or she will know they've been met. How will you assess individual learning? This section includes tips for creating tests relevant to desired outcomes. While creating items for written tests can be tricky—a number of tools in this section address that—there is more to assessing learning than written tests. Note in this section the material that addresses application exercises and performance- or skills-based assessments in addition to more traditional forms of testing.

A tip: A common design error is treating tests and other assessments as afterthoughts: Designers complete lesson plans, visuals, and participant workbooks, and then sift back through it all in search of test questions. Design the tests first, based on the objectives, and *then* design the instruction.

Tip: Why Test?

Contributed by Stephanie Freeman

"As trainers, we have no real way of knowing learning has occurred unless we evaluate our learners in some way. Most of us might know that tests aid in improving instruction, although we may not remember exactly how they do this, or how to make the most of our learners' test results. In crafting tests, consider the ways in which they can be used to do more than just obtain a score on a particular question. There are six ways, outlined below, in which tests aid in improving instruction."

Stephanie Freeman

1. Discovering Gaps in Learning

Much data can be gleaned from looking at test results. Learners performing poorly on a particular question, or set of questions dealing with a particular objective, may signify a "gap" in learning. This could be due to a number of factors, including instruction. The trainer can then take time to review the material in which the learners were weak.

2. Reinforcing Learning

As learners study for their end-of-module tests or other exams, they review the material that they have been taught in class. If you test your learners appropriately during the course, they will be better prepared for a comprehensive exam occurring at the end of the course.

3. Evaluating Methods of Instruction

The usefulness of tests as feedback for the trainer cannot be underestimated. Reviewing test results can help determine how well the class was taught. Suppose, for instance, you are offering a multi-module course taught by different instructors. Compare learner performance on individual sections of a comprehensive examination with end-of-module or end-of-course performance. Poor learner performance on a particular section on the comprehensive exam could be an indicator of a problem with a trainer.

4. Providing an Incentive for Learning

By and large, when learners know that a test is approaching, they will study. The incentive to do well can foster a healthy competition among learners. The main concern is to be careful not to "teach the test"; in other words, don't emphasize test performance to the exclusion of everything else.

5. Providing a Basis for Assigning Grades

Some organizations and professions (nursing, for example) require comprehensive examinations at the conclusion of certain courses. This is meant to ensure that those learners who achieve a passing score have successfully completed some standardized training program. In most cases, the grade learners make on their end-of-course tests should accurately reflect how much they learned in the course. For example, if learners did not have to pass a state's comprehensive examination at the completion of Basic Law Enforcement Training, there would be no uniform standard for police recruits statewide. Training institutions would deliver radically different training programs and there would be no way to ensure that learners from different schools measured up to the same standard.

6. Furnishing a Basis for Selection and Guidance

For some organizations, employees seeking a promotion must take an exam. Passing that exam is part of the eligibility requirements for the promotion. In training, testing serves a similar purpose. Reading comprehension tests prior to the beginning of a course show which learners may be in need of tutoring or extra assistance. Poor performance on written or performance tests during a course can help weed out learners who are unable to meet the standards.

Tool 19. Tie Test Items to Objectives

Contributed by Saul Carliner, Ph.D.

"The only appropriate test questions—and training activities and exercises, for that matter—are the ones that emerge directly from the objectives. Although other questions and exercises might entertain learners, because they do not directly relate to the objectives, they ultimately distract learners from the purpose at hand. The action verb in the objective suggests the question word that should be used. The rest of the objective usually suggests the rest of the question, as shown in these examples."

Saul Carliner

Objective	Sample Test Question/Assessment Activity
Match the countries with their capitals.	Match the country with its capital 1. France 1. Douala 2. Cameroon 2. Brasilia 3. Japan 3. Paris 4. Thailand 4. Bangkok 5. Brazil 5. Tokyo
Name the key steps in the instructional design process according to Dick and Carey.	Name the key steps in the instructional design process, according to Dick and Carey. (Note that there's no change.)
Describe at least three key benefits to small businesses of the X35 copier.	Martin Industries, which has thirty-five employees and $1.2m annual revenues, has decided to replace its copiers. Gina Loprieno, the office manager, has invited you to make a presentation to the company in an effort to win the business. During the question-and-answer period, Gina comments, "This seems like a great copier, but one that's better suited to a company that's much larger than ours. Why should we consider what seems to be more copier than we need?"

Objective	Sample Test Question/Assessment Activity
Using only the wordless instructions, install the desktop PC within 15 minutes and with-out errors.	Perform the following task: Install the desktop PC in the box provided. You may use the instructions included in the box. You have just received the package with the new desktop computer. Install it. **(Trainer:** Use this checklist when observing the performer and check off each box as the user performs it (or indicate that the user did not perform the task: (1) Unpack the box; (2) Identify components; (3) Attach keyboard to system unit.)
Using effectiveness criteria provided in class, recognize an effectively written performance plan.	On the following pages are samples of three performance plans. Indicate below which of the three are effective, according to the criteria discussed in class. **(Trainer:** You might develop an observation list to check off criteria mentioned in the response.)
Given a business case, evaluate the potential opportunity for e-commerce.	Read the following case. Afterward, evaluate the potential opportunity for e-commerce. Specifically name the criteria used in the evaluation. **(Trainer:** You might develop an observation list to check off criteria mentioned in the response. Leave room for criteria developed by the learner.)

Tool 20. Checklist for Culturally Unbiased Test Item Construction

Contributed by Karl Kapp, Ph.D.

For each test item that you create, answer the following questions. If you answer "No" to any of the questions, you will need to rewrite the test item to ensure that it does not contain biased language or content.

Is the question precise when referring to people?	Yes	No
Does the question avoid associating a gender with a profession?	Yes	No
Does the question avoid labeling a behavior/trait as belonging to one gender?	Yes	No
Does the question avoid clinical terms for labeling people?	Yes	No
Does the question avoid classifying people by illness or age?	Yes	No
Does the question avoid culturally specific references?	Yes	No
Does the question avoid unfairly mixing gender terms?	Yes	No
Does the question avoid unfairly describing a population or person?	Yes	No
Does the question avoid language that implies sexual orientation and/or innuendos?	Yes	No

Choosing a Delivery Format

New technologies and approaches have broadened the training horizon from the traditional instructor-led classroom method of delivering instruction. Here are two tools to help with decision making in approaching a new training project.

Tool 21. Delivery Selection Flowchart

Contributed by Don Clark

This chart offers guidance in choosing between myriad approaches to delivering training, from traditional classroom-based format to job aids, mentoring, and e-learning.

Tool 22. Traditional or "E"? Or Both?

Here is a table outlining some decision checkpoints in choosing among various technology-supported—or traditional—training delivery methods. The table shows decision points in the first column, and delivery options in the rest.

Asynchronous—Typically defined as stand-alone tutorials offered via the web or by CD. Learners can access training independently. Opportunities for learner interaction and collaboration can be provided via the use of asynchronous technologies such as discussion boards, blogs, and wikis.

Facilitated Asynchronous—Learners can access the course anytime; an instructor is available to guide and participate in online discussions, direct learners to content, and provide online coaching.

Synchronous—Virtual Classroom: An online session with learners and instructor present at the same time. Sessions are held via virtual classroom technologies such as Elluminate or WebEx.

Synchronous—Physical Classroom. Traditional approach to training with learners and instructor present in classroom together.

Another option is also to blend different approaches. For instance, learners may access some asynchronous content online, then meet in a synchronous session for real-time discussion or role play.

Delivery Method	Asynchronous	Facilitated Asynchronous	Synchronous Virtual Classroom	Synchronous Physical Classroom
Stable Content	X	X	X	X
Need to deliver quickly	X	X	X	
Content changes frequently		X	X	X
Objectives require collaboration	X	X	X	X
Objectives require real-time collaboration			X	X
Need for 24/7 availability	X			
Need for self-paced approach	X			
Need for consistent messaging	X			
Large target audience	X	X		
Learners are geographically dispersed	X	X	X	
Objectives require live interaction with instructor		X	X	

Course Design and Lesson Planning

In this "blueprinting" stage we begin to lay out the basic structure and overall approach to our course. The first tool here is for those working on a design team. It helps outline the information that will be handed off to an instructional designer. The remaining tools are outlines for drafting basic lesson plans and creating storyboards for use in developing e-learning programs.

Tool 23. Course Design Worksheet

Contributed by Jerry Linnins

Here is a comprehensive, detailed design worksheet. The completed example shown here, provided by contributor Jerry Linnins as used by his own organization, shows the detailed foundation of designing a course on "Introduction to Training Course Development" utilizing the relevant phases of the ADDIE model. The finished worksheet is then forwarded to the instructional designer, who uses this as the blueprint for creating the course.

Course Title, "G" Number Owner, Contact Information, Responsible Function

Introduction to Training Course Development, G-PM027

David Smith /Jerry Linnins, Office of Capital Projects Skill Development

Learning Outcome: (brief, generalized statement of purpose; approximately 25 words phrased as a sentence or paragraph; focus on what a course graduate should be able to DO)

Introduces participants to the theory, tools, and techniques necessary to use the ADDIE (analyze-design-develop-implement-evaluate) model, complete their Course Developers Work Breakdown Structure (WBS) activities, and acquire the Course Developer skills outlined in the 1998 International Board of Standards for Training Performance and Instruction (IBSTPI) Instructional Design Standards. This course lays a framework for participants to move from merely acquiring Course Developer skills (need assistance when performing) to competency (performs on own) and ultimately to proficiency (performs efficiently).

What This Course Prepares the Learner to Do

1.1. **Analysis**—Determine training needs; plan costs and schedules
1.2. **Course Design**—Create an instructional strategy
1.3. **Course Development**—Create instructional products/conduct a course pilot
1.4. **Evaluation**—Create a Course Evaluation Plan/Audit, Part A-C
1.5. **Implementation/Delivery**—Course delivery will be addressed by a separate "Train-the-Trainer" Course.

Roles/Personnel Who Should Attend Course

This course is intended *primarily* for those assigned as Course Developers. Others who may find it beneficial include, but are not limited to, training coordinators, instructors/trainers, various managers, and the staff members of the Office of Capital Projects Skill Development. It may also be offered to vendors/contractors providing skill development products and services to Capital Projects.

Listing of Knowledge, Tasks, Skills (KTS) to Be Covered by Course

Be as specific as possible. Think of what you want a graduate of this course to know, to be able to do, the person's attitude on the job, and what tools/equipment/resources will be needed. Use additional copies of this form as may be needed to completely identify the required knowledge, technical skills, and soft skills.

Note: The KTS identified below are merely foundational and are intended to prepare participants to move from Course Developer skill acquisition to competence and ultimately to proficiency.

Technical Knowledge	Tools and/or Equipment Skills	Performance Skills (Soft Skills)
Instructional Systems Design (ISD/ADDIE) theory and practices (analysis, design, development, implementation, and evaluation)	Designers Edge Course Planning Software	Communication skills (general writing, verbal, technical writing, and presentation/public speaking)
Course Developers WBS process for course development, funding, and delivery	Guide to Course Development and Implementation (WBS)	Active listening skills (empathy, Inquiry, reflection, advocacy)
Training Audits (purpose, use for, etc.) Parts A-C	ISD Workbooks 1 to 5 (includes various templates, worksheets, decision aids)	Observational skills (ability to see both "forest" and "trees" and maintain a situational awareness)
Subject-Matter Expertise in some relevant discipline associated with Capital Projects areas of responsibility	Training Audit Guide (Parts A-C)	Interpersonal skills (consensus, teamwork, negotiation, conflict resolution, etc.)

Technical Knowledge	Tools and/or Equipment Skills	Performance Skills (Soft Skills)
Basic computer literacy (word processing, Internet, intranet, email, presentations, spread-sheet, etc.)	MSWord, PowerPoint	Learning skills (feel, think, observe, perform)
Code of Conduct for Course Developers	MS Excel	Leadership (task and maintenance)
Instructional Design standards (IBSTPI, Office of Skill Development, Baldridge, ISO9000, etc.)	Project 140 website	Management skills (plan, organize, staff, direct, and control)
Adult learning principles and practices	Budget Form website	Interviewing skills
Designers Edge course planning software theory, process, and features	Designers Edge Training Tutorial	Consulting skills (contract, plan, deliver, evaluate) (entry, contract, conclude, exit)
Performance Improvement principles and models	MS PowerPoint	Coaching and Mentoring skills
Training theory and practices (purpose, design, constraints)	Relevant policy or guidance statements from the Office of Skill Development	Facilitation skills (meeting management, group dynamics, etc.)
Communication theory and techniques	Training Media (audiovisual, overheads, slides, projectors, laptops, flip charts, etc.)	Advanced reading skills (ability to read technical, academic material and digests)
Testing and performance assessment theory and techniques	Course Design Packages	
Basic business literacy (understanding of Caltrans, Capital Projects, and/or specific function (ESC, Design, etc.)	Other tools and techniques as may be identified, procured, or mandated to support course development	
Project management theory and practices		
Planning theory and techniques		

Audience Profile

Learner Characteristics

This section is to be used to capture a profile of those expected to attend the course. Any assumptions you may make about who is attending, what they already know or can do, special needs, education or skill level expected, etc., should be documented. Three categories of such information include:

- **General characteristics:** basic assumptions about those attending (physically fit, experience level, role)

- **Entry behaviors:** prerequisites; things attendees need to bring with them to be successful in the course

- **Style/Preference:** known norms, things audience liked from previous training, delivery preferences, etc.

Note: It is anticipated that <u>initially</u> the Office of Skill Development may have little or no control over who attends this course as participants are selected by their own functions (ESC, Design, etc.). This may result in widely varying audience characteristics, entry behaviors, and an inability to enforce desired prerequisites. This should change over time as the Skill Development Plan becomes institutionalized.

General Characteristics

- Employees from one of the seven Capital Projects functions (Environmental, Design, Right of Way, Traffic Operations, Project Management, ESC, and Construction)

- Some experience/understanding of the role for which they will be developing courses (Planner, Engineer, etc.)

- Some experience in Caltrans

- Most are college graduates and hold professional certifications in their fields

Entry Behaviors

- Minimal exposure to the Instructional Systems Design Model and/or developing training

- Minimal exposure to Designers Edge course planning software

- Minimal exposure to adult learning/training theory, principles, and techniques

- Basic literacy skills (read, write, math)

- Computer literate (PC)

- Limited understanding of the process used to date for creating the Skill Development Plan

- Volunteered for course developer role or was hired specifically for that role

Style/Learning Preferences

- Culturally accustomed to classroom, instructor-mediated (lecture) instruction and training

- Used to working independently and not as part of a larger design team

- Not generally accustomed to self-paced learning events

- Expect all learning styles to be present in class. However, expect a preponderance of kinesthetic learners. This may affect the pacing, sequencing, and level of facilitation required.

- Culturally, most have taken a "product" orientation. This may impact the instruction of a course that is theory-based and focuses on teaching process. The rush to get product may interfere with the need to first master the process.

Course Size	*Length*	*Expected Throughput*
Recommended: 12 (fewer impacts the level of interaction in class and more may limit participants ability to get enough practice/feedback	5.5 days (8:00–4:30, one-hr. lunch)	Annual: 20 to 50. Urgent Need: 50 (skill development plan start-up)

Priority for Attending (Who Should Attend/When?):

First priority should be for those hired/selected to actually develop courses for their individual functions. Others may attend as determined by the Office of Capital Projects Skill Development.

How Should This Course Be Delivered and Why?

Be as specific as possible regarding:

- Who will deliver it?

- Where will they deliver it?

- When will they deliver it?

- How they will deliver it? ·

Here are some examples:

Vendor delivered (initially with a planned transition to Caltrans personnel)

One-week intensive classroom and computer lab followed by self-paced practice by participants. This practice period will then be followed up by a one half-day performance feedback, action planning and evaluation session.

Instructor-mediated classroom instruction supplemented with instructor-facilitated exercises, computer laboratory, student-led discussions and self-paced learning application exercises

Vendor-provided tutorial for Designers Edge and other internally provided resources (workbooks, guides, websites, etc.)

Why Should It Be Delivered This Way?

Be as specific as possible regarding:

- Use the Training Media Selection Chart

- Note any preferences/special needs

- Note any constraints or barriers that require this delivery format

Here are some examples:

This course is an **introduction** to the development of effective and efficient training. It outlines a process to be used, provides a wide variety of tools and performance support materials. Additionally, it gives each participant a chance to practice those skills they will be using on the job. Significant amounts of feedback and learning guidance are provided by course materials and assigned instructors. Participants will walk out of the class having acquired new skills (or new skill levels). With additional practice and feedback, they will become competent Course

Developers. Over time, with supportive management, they will become proficient in the development of training courses. Some will even become accomplished performers.

Because of the urgency with which courses need to be developed, the desire to have developed courses meet identified standards, and the relatively low experience level entering participants have to the field of training, it is felt this "boot camp" approach is the most effective.

Use of the Designers Edge course planning software has been shown to reduce the amount of time it takes non-training experts producing courses and courseware. Creation and maintenance of the Project 140 website, the building of a library of course design resources at that site, and the active involvement of the staff of the Office of Capital Projects Skill Development are likewise helpful.

The use of one half-day performance feedback, action planning, and evaluation session was helpful in the design of this course following a Course Developers workshop. It should prove helpful to the further development, improvement of this course's current design.

Creating Lesson Plans

The design phase of ADDIE includes the drafting of the overall instructional plan, to be fleshed out into instructor guides in the Development phase. The first item in this section, Tool 24, is a two-part tool for managing the lesson planning process. Following that are templates for creating lesson plans. The choice of which to use is a matter of preference: Tool 25 provides a worksheet format, while Tool 26 is an outline approach to lesson planning. I tend to prefer the simplicity of Tool 25 when designing a lesson solely for my own use, and a more in-depth approach when working on material that will eventually form the basis for a facilitator guide that will be used by another trainer.

Tool 24. Lesson Plan Checklist and Content Matrix for Lesson Planning

Contributed by Peggy Schaefer

This tool has two parts. The first is an outline for synthesizing information from steps such as analysis and writing objectives, and checking off steps in lesson plan development. This tool was developed for use by a law enforcement academy, where development is often done by a committee that includes a number of subject-matter experts (SMEs). As shown in the appendix to this tool, tasks and skills detailed in the analysis phase are configured into a matrix, which the SMEs committee then uses to help with prioritizing and sequencing the lesson. You may be entering the design phase with this information so would then perhaps choose to skip section A. Item B.6 references the development of instructor guides, which is covered in-depth in Chapter 3: Develop.

Lesson Plan Development Checklist

Development Tasks Date Completed

A. **Analyze** the specific tasks associated with the subject and prioritize when the tasks will be taught in your lesson plan.

   1. Select SMEs for matrix brainstorming session _____

   2. Conduct meeting and select tasks for matrix _____

   3. Complete matrix (Appendix) and disseminate to respondents _____

   4. Collect matrix and quantify results _____

B. **Build** the lesson plan.

   1. Write coherent, measurable, concrete objectives _____

   2. Conduct literature review: magazine articles, books, journals, web _____

   3. Synthesize the gathered materials and select best sources that support the training objectives _____

   4. Write lesson plan _____

   5. Develop visuals, slides, handouts _____

   6. Create instructor guide _____

C. Cite sources!

  1. Complete reference list, citing all references used _____

Appendix: Content Matrix for Lesson Planning

Here is an example of a matrix developed for a meeting with subject-matter experts in defining content and priorities for "Vehicle Stop Tactics for Patrol Officers" training. Information from this matrix is used in developing the instructional plan as outlined in Tool 24.

Instructions: Using the scale at the top of the grid, indicate the relative importance of each of the following skills/tasks for the training segment concerning vehicle stop training. Also, please indicate any other tasks associated with traffic stops that you or other officers may be deficient in that should be a part of this training block of instruction.

Example: Vehicle Stop Tactics for Patrol Officers					
Task	**Most Important**	**Somewhat Important**	**Neutral**	**Not Very Important**	**Not Needed**
Identify the traffic violation, i.e., reason to make the stop.					
Mentally prepare for the vehicle stop.					
Communicate effectively on the police radio and correctly operate equipment.					
Safely position patrol vehicle for known and unknown vehicle stops.					
Verbally and physically control vehicle occupants during vehicle stops.					
Safely stop vans, tractor-trailers and motorcycles.					
Other:					

Tool 25. Lesson Plan Template A: Overview Format

Contributed by Jennifer Henczel

Lesson Plan Template A: Overview Format

Topic of my lesson:

Time:

Learning Objective:
What do I want my learners to know or be able to do as a result of this lesson?

Hook:
How will I open the lesson and connect the learners to the material?

Why should they be interested in this lesson?

Pre-Test:
What will I do to find out what the learners already know about the topic?

Participatory Learning:
What teaching and learning activities will take place to help my students learn?

What will the learners do?	What will I do?	Teaching aids/resources	Time

Post-Test:
How will I and my learners know that learning has occurred?

Summary:

Tool 26. Lesson Plan Template B: Outline Format

Contributed by Don Clark

Note that items within brackets are notes for and may be edited by the course designer.

Lesson Title

Course Time: [150 minutes]	Learner Outcome: [This is not read to the learners but instead use the Objective and Course Requirements below for that purpose. This outcome is to help the developer build the lesson plan.]
	Task: [Starting with a verb, describe the observable performance or behavior.]
	Condition: [Describe the actual conditions under which the task will occur or be observed.]
	Standard: [State the level of acceptable performance of the task in terms of quantity, quality, time limitations, etc.]
Time:[5 min.]	Introduction: [Introduce yourself with name, authority (why learners should listen to you), some humor, special instructions, information on the facilities, etc.]
Time: [3 min.]	Objective: [Help learners visualize a clear goal, such as what this learning will help them to achieve. What will they be able to do in the future? Why are they spending their time in this class?]
Time: [2 min.]	Course Requirements: [What must they do to pass the course? How will they know they can perform the task correctly?]
Time: [5 min.]	Course Description: [Give the big picture (global). List the details in the instructional outline (liner). Some people will prefer large-scale concepts(overall view of the material), while others prefer one-step-at-a-time instructions.
	Stimulate recall of prior learning: Show how this lesson is built on prior lessons or pre-course requirements.]

Instructional Outline: [Enter body of lesson in outline form below. Normally, there would be about four learning points for each hour or two of instruction, depending on difficulty, as the learners need time to "absorb" the information.]

Time: [25 min.]   First Learning Point:

Time: [15 min.]   Second Learning Point:

Time: [20 min.]   Third Learning Point:

Time: [15 min.]   Fourth Learning Point:

Time: [10 min.]   [Elicit performance (practice) and provide feedback.]

Time: [10 min.]   Review: [After one or two hours of class, depending on complexity of the material, perform reflection or review activities.

       Reflection is an active process (the doer must think). Use pairs, groups, and individual activities.

       Reviews can also be done as activities.]

Time: [10 min.]   Evaluation: [Know what behaviors are to be looked for and how they are rated. These behaviors MUST support the learner outcomes (learning objectives).]

       Retention and Transfer: [How will you ensure that the training will be used on the job? There is no use in training if people are not going to use it (or lose what they do not use).]

Storyboarding Tools

A critical step in e-learning design phase is storyboarding, or "dummying up," a sample of the finished program. The storyboard is, essentially, a very detailed script, and in moving from the design to development phases designers may work with storyboards as they move from bare-bones outlines to fully fleshed out, detailed scripts. This section offers some options for storyboarding.

Tip: Storyboarding e-Learning with PowerPoint

Readers of my books *e-Learning Solutions on a Shoestring* and *Better Than Bullet Points* know that I am a proponent of using PowerPoint® for creating e-learning. Regardless of the authoring tool you choose, Power-Point can still be a good tool for storyboarding: It is something most trainers already have and already know how to use. I have also found that providing a program overview in PowerPoint, as opposed to a written script, helps clients get a better idea of the final look of a program in development. PowerPoint's slide sorter view as shown in Figure 2.1 gives a bird's-eye view of a program, helping the designer see where there may be too many sequential text-heavy screens, and allows for easy rearrangement of material. The speaker notes area beneath each slide offers room to enter directions for programmers and script for narrators. This is shown in Figure 2.2.

Figure 2.1. Slide Sorter View Offers "Bird's Eye" View

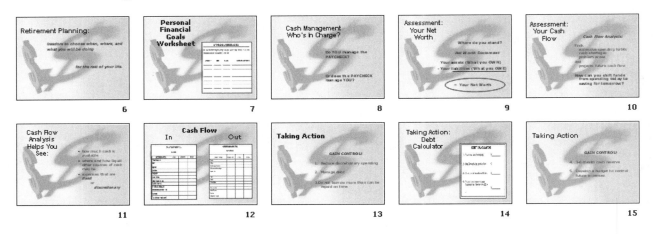

Figure 2.2. Speaker Notes Area Used for Storyboarding

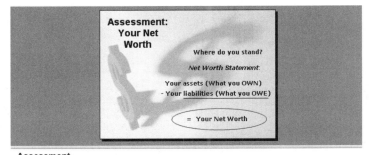

Tool 27. Storyboard Template A: PowerPoint Format

Contributed by Karl Kapp, Ph.D.

Here is a template for more detailed storyboarding. This one is offered as a PowerPoint template, allowing for easy insertion of graphics and, as noted above in the comments about PowerPoint's slide sorter view, allows for easy rearrangement of slides.

Web Storyboard			
Project Name:	**Current Screen ID:**	**Page of**	**Navigation/Hyperlinks:**
Web Media Elements: ☑ ☐ Animation ☐ Graphics ☐ Text ☐ Video ☐ Voice ☐ Music ☐ Sound Effects **Date:**			Enter information about the navigation on the screen.
This sections is where the actual screen is sketched or copied into the storyboard			**Programming Notes:** Enter notes to the programmer here. **Asset List:** Here is where you indicate the file names for graphic and sound files.

Tool 28. Storyboard Template B: Word Format

This template is formatted as a Word document. While I find it easier to work with PowerPoint, which allows me to get a sense of the overall look of the final program, this format is more traditional and is widely used by e-learning developers.

Program	Module
Date	Screen #
Writer	Programmer
Version #	Revision #

Screen Description
Graphics
Multimedia
Text
Voiceover
Links

Quiz/Feedback for Learners	
Music/Sound FX	
Notes/Special Instructions	
Reviewer	Review Date

Cost and Time Estimators

Most industry figures on costs and development time work from the assumption of an "hour" of instruction. This is a tricky starting point, particularly with online training programs. Learners working alone on self-paced online programs may vary widely in the time it takes them to complete a given piece of instruction, depending on any number of factors from their reading speed to the number of interruptions they face. A detailed simulation may result in "an hour" of instruction, but take exponentially more time to develop than dozens of text-based minimally interactive screens of content (which aren't "e-learning" anyway, but that's another book). Costs are dependent on a number of factors, and estimating final expenses is less a matter of finding hard-and-fast rules as making educated guesses. Tool 29 offers a broad-brush view of costs associated with a training project; see Tools 30 and 31 for factoring in mitigating concerns and issues that can affect price and development time.

Tool 29. "Rule of Thumb" Costs for Training

These are meant as very general guidelines, offered in U.S. dollar prices current with industry literature as of July 2007. See the note in the introduction to this section regarding the matter of an "hour" of online instruction.

	Instructor-Led/ Classroom (ILT)	**Asynchronous e-Learning**
Cost for development of one hour of instruction	40 hours @ $60/hour = $2,400	200 hours (for basic program with minimal interactivity) @$75 = $15,000 For interactive multimedia: 500 hours @ $75 = $37,500
Instructor salary; add 20% for burdened costs: payroll tax, insurance, other benefits	Assumed base salary: $60,000/year/Burdened costs: $12,000/Total salary: $72,00 At 240 work days per year, 8-hour work day, instructor salary is $300/day; $37.50/ hour	$0
Learner salary; add 20% for burdened costs of payroll tax, insurance, other benefits	Assumed base salary: $40,000/year; Burdened costs: $8,000; Total salary: $48,000; At 240 work days per year, 8-hour work day, learner salary is $200/day or $25/hour	Same, but seat time should be at least half of that associated with ILT (for instance, material is condensed, training day does not include down time for breaks, lunch, warm-ups, icebreakers, etc., as with traditional classroom)
Instructor travel for one-day training session (travel requires half-day before session, evening in hotel, day attending training, another evening in hotel, and half-day returning home)	If applicable, assume $450 airfare, 2 nights lodging @$140, $160 per diem for transportation and meals; Total travel: $770	$0

	Instructor-Led/ Classroom (ILT)	Asynchronous e-Learning
Learner travel costs for 1-day training session (travel requires half-day before session, evening in hotel, day attending training, another evening in hotel, and half-day returning home)	If applicable, assume $450 airfare, 2 nights lodging @$140, $160 per diem for transportation and meals; Total travel per learner: $770	$0
Site costs	Wear and tear/use of company training classroom and equipment = $200/day	Hosting on company intranet = $0; External hosting: $10-$200/month
*Administrative Costs	Varies (see below)	Varies (see below)

*Note: a factor not priced out in this tool is that of administrative costs related to a particular training event. This has perhaps the widest variation of any factor. An organization using classroom management software to handle registrations, verify attendance, and send reminders may spend US $15,000 a year to manage all training events for all employees. The price breakdown could then be, theoretically, as low as pennies per learner per event, which would add very little to the instructor-led training costs in our example above. Employing staff to handle administrative tasks "by hand" would likely incur much higher per-learner costs. Similarly, with an e-learning approach, a hyperlink to an e-mail completion notice costs nothing, while utilizing a six- (or even seven-) figure learning management system (LMS) would drive administrative costs up significantly. Be sure to include administrative costs appropriate for your organization in estimations of your project.

Example

Midwestern company with 500 sales reps who need to attend a one-day sales strategies workshop.

If held in classroom, training will be held at central training site to which the sales reps will travel.

Details	Instructor-Led Classroom	Asynchronous e-Learning
Number of sessions: Course has expected 3-year life span, there are 500 employees and turnover is 20% (100 people) annually. First year learners = 500, plus 100 more each in years 2 and 3. Total learners over the 3 years = 700 With 15 learners per class, 47 sessions will be required.	47	0
Materials	700 workbooks @ $4 = $2,800	$0
Site costs	Wear and tear/use of company training classroom and equipment = $200/day	Hosting on company intranet = $0
TOTAL delivery costs	8-hour training day **Instructor** Salary: 8 hours salary + 4 hours preparation time = $450 Instructor Travel: (assume here that instructor is in central location and learners travel to training site) $0; Instructor costs $450 × 47 sessions = $21,150 **Learner**—due to travel will be off work site for training day *plus* half day before and after training *Salary: $800;* Travel: $770; Cost per learner = $1,970 × 700 learners = $1,379,000 **Site costs:** 47 days @ $200 = $9,400	For 4-hour online program **Learner:** Salary $200; Travel: $0; Cost per learner: $200 × 700 learners = $1,400 **Site costs:** $0

Details	Instructor-Led Classroom	Asynchronous e-Learning
	Materials $2,800 **Total delivery cost:** Instructor costs: $21,150; Learner costs: $1,379,000; Site costs: $9,400; Materials costs: $2,800 = $1,412,350	**Materials:** $0 **Total delivery cost:** = $1,400
TOTAL development costs of delivering an 8-hour training program; time cut to 4 hours by delivering online	8 hours of instruction @ $2,400 = $19,200 (does not include costs of updating over 3 years)	4 hours of basic instruction @ $15,000 = $60,000 (does not include cost of updating over 3 years)
TOTAL COST:	$1,431,550	$61,400

Tool 30. Training Design Time Estimate Worksheet

Contributed by Gary Lear

This table includes some of the "people factors" involved in a training design project. Expertise (or lack thereof), the level of client involvement, and the definition of "complete" can all affect design time.

Variables	Level of Effort for Design		
	Low	**Medium**	**High**
who			
1. The designer's knowledge and skills related to instructional design	☐ Extensive knowledge and skills	☐ Moderate knowledge and skills	☐ Minimal knowledge and skills
2. The designer's knowledge of the training subject matter	☐ Extensive knowledge	☐ Some knowledge	☐ No knowledge
3. The size and complexity of the target training group	☐ Small, homogeneous	☐ Medium, moderately complex	☐ Large, complex
4. The designer's and the client's track records for sticking to plans	☐ Always stick	☐ Sometimes stick	☐ Never stick
What			
5. The number of instruction modules	☐ Few (5 modules)	☐ Several (8 modules)	☐ Many (12 modules)
6. The elements included in the training materials	☐ Participant materials only	☐ An instructor manual and a participant manual	☐ An instructor manual, a participant manual, overheads, and/or job aids

Variables	Level of Effort for Design		
	Low	**Medium**	**High**
7. The client's or organization's expectations regarding packaging	☐ Minimal (produced in-house)	☐ Modest (desktop publishing)	☐ Extensive (professionally produced)
8. What is considered final product	☐ Designer completes first draft, client does rest	☐ Designer completes up to the pilot	☐ Designer completes all drafts, finalizes after pilot
How			
9. Data collection	☐ A focus group made up of a few well-informed people	☐ A focus group and a few interviews	☐ Several focus groups and several interviews
10. The designer's interaction	☐ Deals directly with the top decision-maker	☐ Deals with more than one level of decision-maker	☐ Deals with a complex labor-management committee
11. The client's level of involvement	☐ Approves general direction and final draft	☐ Reviews and approves key materials	☐ Review and approves all materials
12. The program's degree of interactivity	☐ Minimal	☐ Moderate	☐ Extensive
Effort			
	Low	**Medium**	**High**
Total Boxes Checked	____ × 1 = ____(a)	____ × 2 = ____(b)	____ × 3 = ____(c)

_____ (a+b+c) × _____ (Total Training Hours for the Program)

= _____ (Total Design Hours)

Tool 31. e-Learning Design Time Estimator

Contributed by Pete Blair

Trainer and instructional designer Pete Blair provides an interactive time estimator calculator, for free, on the homepage of his website www.peteblair. com. The calculator allows for more specific quantifying of the items below, but this chart can give an idea of the factors that will affect e-learning design time, and will prove helpful in conversations you may need to have with management regarding time estimates. Development of complex interactions and new graphics are more heavily weighted than other items.

Factor		
Expert	Content Expertise	Low
Expert	Instructional Design Expertise	Entry Level
One	Number of Design-Development Team Members	Five +
Low	Level of Interaction	Complex Simulation
None	Number of New Graphics	1 per screen

Development time

Project Planning

In planning a training project, whether you are a "lone ranger" or working with a team of graphic artists and web developers, it's very easy to overlook something. Scrambling too late to order participant materials—or arrange for the trainer's plane ticket—can be avoided by use of a checklist or project planning tool. There is software available for instructional design projects, and there is general project management software available (such as MS Project). The choice of what to use depends on your preferences, the learning curve the products require, and the complexity of your project. This section offers Tool 32, a quick-and-dirty project risk assessment tool from Lou Russell. Tools 33 and 34 then offer examples of a basic overview approach to planning both e-learning and classroom training projects. These are followed by Tool 35, an in-depth Excel®-based adaptation of Tool 34's outline as detailed by contributor Results Through Training.

Tool 32. Training Project Risk Assessment: "Quick and Dirty Risk"

Contributed by Lou Russell

This very quick technique is used to help everyone involved understand how risky this project is, compared to others. In addition, the higher the calculated number at the end, the more time you must spend managing (planning, organizing, and controlling) rather than just doing (ADDIE) the project.

When starting a project, gather as many project stakeholders (people who have a stake in the success of your project) together and ask them to write down a number for each of the following:

Size—How "big" is this project or how long will it take relative to others you and your team have done?

Rated 1(small)—10(large)

Structure—How stable are the requirements? In other words, how many different people are involved? How likely is it that the requirements will change over the life of the project?

Rated 1(fixed)—10(undefined)

Technology—How understood is the technology relative to others you and your team have expertise in?

Rated 1(old)—10(new)

To calculate: Average these numbers (add together and divide by 3) and share with each other.

- Discuss why you chose different numbers.

- Adjust your project plan based on what you have learned about the risk.

- Hold more or less time to manage your project.

Tool 33. e-Learning Project Plan Outline

Adapted from a worksheet by Kevin Kruse

Here's a basic outline for an e-learning project. See Tool 35 for an example of using a more detailed Excel-based approach to managing a project; the simple outline is really a basis for the more detailed planning shown in that example.

Task	Who	By When	Status
Analysis			
Acquire content knowledge			
Perform job and task analysis			
Perform instructional analysis; create/ revise objectives			
Create competency map			
Write criterion-referenced test items			
Develop instructional strategies			
Develop performance support strategies			
Develop detailed course outline			
Prepare design and project management documents			
Design			
Design user interface and application graphics standards			
Design functional elements			
Design application architecture			
Create detailed storyboards			
Create sample lesson and performance support module			
Create preliminary learner guide			
Develop			
Construct and develop instructional content			

Task	Who	By When	Status
Script and program functional elements			
Embed links to service documentation			
Create graphics and animation sequences			
Create 3-D model and scripts			
Set alternate language properties			
Write documentation for maintenance			
Write help materials			
Create any supplemental learning guides			
Evaluation			
Test form and function			
Test usability			
Validate content accuracy and completeness			
Revise as necessary			
Implementation			
Prepare media for installation and shipment (if CD)			
Assist client with implementation issues			

Tool 34. Classroom Training Project Planning Outline

Contributed by Results Through Training
(www.RTTWorks.com)

Analyze	By When	Who?	Status
Meet with client to define needs			
Conduct needs survey with target audience			
Prepare needs assessment report; review with client			
Design			
Write objectives			
Develop assessments/test items			
Determine delivery format			
Write blueprint design document/storyboard			
Gain approval on design document			
Draft content for workbook			
Develop			
Write trainer notes and agenda			
Create visuals, slides, posters, design flip charts			
Develop participant materials, workbooks, and handouts			
Review trainer notes and gain approval			
Proofread and send final edits to all documents			
Prep masters for reproduction			
Final proof pre-pilot			
Pilot-test materials			
Determine edits based on pilot.			
Make final edits based on pilot			
Submit final materials			

From Analysis to Evaluation: Tools, Tips, and Techniques for Trainers.
Copyright © 2008 by John Wiley & Sons, Inc. Reproduced by permission of Pfeiffer, an Imprint of Wiley. www.pfeiffer.com

Analyze	By When	Who?	Status
Implement			
Request class roster from client; confirm # people. Record on project schedule			
Create email message for pre-work			
Check inventory of all materials (books, instruments, etc.)			
Make any additional flip charts			
Confirm final number of copies of materials needed.			
Final proof pre-production			
Send message confirming dates, location, pre-work			
Create trainer binder of materials; send to trainer			
Schedule trainer travel; file travel itinerary.			
Materials due back from reproduction			
Proof materials post production/assemble binders			
Send room setup and equipment needs to client			
Pack workbooks, trainer materials			
Ship flip charts and materials			
Confirm receipt of materials by client			
Send final materials to trainer (trainer sheet, directions)			
Teach Workshop			
Process evals/send to client (with roster) and trainer			
Unpack class materials/clean up flips/store			
Email reinforcement message 1			
Email reinforcement message 2			
Email reinforcement message 3			

Analyze	By When	Who?	Status
Email reinforcement message 4			
Check inventory of all materials (books, instruments, etc.)			
Make edits to course materials			
Confirm final number of materials needed			
Final proof pre-production			
Prepare master(s) for reproduction (including covers); verify you have NEWEST version; take to copy facility			
Schedule trainer travel; file travel itinerary			
Materials due back from copy facility			
Proof materials post production/assemble binders			
Send room set up and equipment needs to client (write up instructions for client)			
Pack workbooks, trainer materials and toys; proof			
Ship flips and materials to client			
Process surveys			
Confirm receipt of materials by client			
Proof survey reports			
Make final edits to survey reports			
Prepare surveys for shipping			
Send final materials to trainer (trainer sheet, directions, survey)			
Teach Workshop			
Prepare invoice; log on Project Schedule; update project schedule			
Process evals/send to client (with roster) and trainer, file one set in folder			
Unpack class materials/clean up flips/store			

Analyze	By When	Who?	Status
Evaluate			
Email follow-up message 1			
Follow-up message 2			
Follow-up message 3			
Follow-up survey			
Process follow-up surveys			
Track survey returns; address errors, and solicit missing surveys			

Tool 35. Project Planning Worksheet

The last item in this section is a detailed Excel-based project planning tool developed by RTT Works (www.RTTWorks.com). The example here, based on the outline provided in Tool 33, shows the plan for a course on "negotiation skills ." Items include a detailed list of tasks, time remaining, process owner, and a place for notes. This tool is included on the CD as an Excel file. Plans for three different courses, each differing in some way, are provided , as is a blank planning tool.

While many trainers and designers accustomed to working in a "fly by the seat of your pants" approach may be intimidated by a plan as detailed as this, it can be helpful in laying out projects that will involve multiple people or in managing several projects at once. It is easy, for instance, to forget to ship handouts to a remote location ahead of the training, or to overlook sending follow-up emails to participants. A tool like this is also useful in walking clients through plans for a project—and explaining why development typically takes considerable effort in terms of time and money.

Job No.	Customer	Project	Task	D-Day	D Minus (End no later than (days))	Time Reqd (days)	Start Date	Due Date	RTT Week Start	RTT Week Due	1st Owner	Status/ Notes
2154	Finance	Negotiation skills	Meet with customer to define needs	8/31/2008	75	2	6/15/2008	6/17/2008	#NAME?	#NAME?	CO	
2154	Finance	Negotiation skills	Conduct needs survey with target audience	8/31/2008	65	7	6/20/2008	6/27/2008	#NAME?	#NAME?	CO	
2154	Finance	Negotiation skills	Prepare needs assessment report; review with customer	8/31/2008	60	3	6/29/2008	7/2/2008	#NAME?	#NAME?	CO	
2154	Finance	Negotiation skills	Write Design document	8/31/2008	55	4	7/3/2008	7/7/2008	#NAME?	#NAME?	CO	
2154	Finance	Negotiation skills	Get approval on design document	8/31/2008	50	2	7/10/2008	7/12/2008	#NAME?	#NAME?	CO	
2154	Finance	Negotiation skills	Draft Content for workbook	8/31/2008	45	8	7/9/2008	7/17/2008	#NAME?	#NAME?	CO	
2154	Finance	Negotiation skills	Write Action plan, planner and other handouts	8/31/2008	35	2	7/25/2008	7/27/2008	#NAME?	#NAME?	CO	
2154	Finance	Negotiation skills	Review workbook with customer and gain approval.	8/31/2008	27	2	8/2/2008	8/4/2008	#NAME?	#NAME?	CO	
2154	Finance	Negotiation skills	Write trainer notes and agenda	8/31/2008	25	7	7/30/2008	8/6/2008	#NAME?	#NAME?	CO	
2154	Finance	Negotiation skills	Write visual support masters	8/31/2008	21	2	8/8/2008	8/10/2008	#NAME?	#NAME?	CO	
2154	Finance	Negotiation skills	Review trainer notes and gain approval	8/31/2008	20	2	8/9/2008	8/11/2008	#NAME?	#NAME?	CO	
2154	Finance	Negotiation skills	Proof & final edits to all documents	8/31/2008	16	2	8/13/2008	8/15/2008	#NAME?	#NAME?	CO	
2154	Finance	Negotiation skills	Prep masters for reproduction	8/31/2008	14	7	8/10/2008	8/17/2008	#NAME?	#NAME?	SK	
2154	Finance	Negotiation skills	Create flip charts, slides, and posters	8/31/2008	10	4	8/17/2008	8/21/2008	#NAME?	#NAME?	SK	
2154	Finance	Negotiation skills	Final proof pre-pilot	8/31/2008	7	2	8/22/2008	8/24/2008	#NAME?	#NAME?	CO	
2154	Finance	Negotiation skills	Pilot test materials	8/31/2008	0	1	8/30/2008	8/31/2008	#NAME?	#NAME?	CO	
2154	Finance	Negotiation skills	Determine edits based on pilot.	8/31/2008	-5	3	9/2/2008	9/5/2008	#NAME?		CO	
B1013C	Finance	Communication skills	Request class roster from customer; confirm # people Record on project schedule	10/14/2008	35	1	9/8/2008	9/9/2008			CO	
2154	Finance	Negotiation skills	Make final edits based on pilot	8/31/2008	-15	7	9/8/2008	9/15/2008	#NAME?	#NAME?	CO	
2154	Finance	Negotiation skills	Submit final materials; close project.	8/31/2008	-20	10	9/10/2008	9/20/2008	#NAME?	#NAME?	CO	
B1013C	Finance	Communication skills	Create Email message for prework	10/14/2008	21	1	9/22/2008	9/23/2008	#NAME?	#NAME?	SK	
B1013C	Finance	Communication skills	Check inventory of all materials (books, instruments, etc.)	10/14/2008	21	1	9/22/2008	9/23/2008	#NAME?		SK	
B1013C	Finance	Communication skills	Make flip charts	10/14/2008	21	2	9/21/2008	9/23/2008	#NAME?		SK	
B1013C	Finance	Communication skills	Confirm final number of materials needed.	10/14/2008	20	1	9/23/2008	9/24/2008	#NAME?		CO	
B1013C	Finance	Communication skills	Final proof pre-production	10/14/2008	19	1	9/24/2008	9/25/2008	#NAME?		SK	
B1013C	Finance	Communication skills	Send msg confirming dates, location, prework	10/14/2008	18	2	9/24/2008	9/26/2008	#NAME?		SK	
B1013C	Finance	Communication skills	Prepare Master(s) for reproduction	10/14/2008	18	1	9/25/2008	9/26/2008	#NAME?		SK	
B1013C	Finance	Communication skills	Create Trainer Binder of materials; send to trainer	10/14/2008	17	1	9/26/2008	9/27/2008	#NAME?		SK	
B1013C	Finance	Communication skills	Schedule trainer travel; File travel itinerary.	10/14/2008	16	1	9/27/2008	9/28/2008	#NAME?		TR	
B1013C	Finance	Communication skills	Materials due back from reproduction	10/14/2008	16	0	9/28/2008	9/28/2008	#NAME?		SK	
B1013C	Finance	Communication skills	Proof materials post production/assemble binders	10/14/2008	15	1	9/28/2008	9/29/2008	#NAME?		SK	
B1013C	Finance	Communication skills	Send room set up and equipment needs to Customer	10/14/2008	14	1	9/29/2008	9/30/2008	#NAME?		SK	
B1013C	Finance	Communication skills	Pack workbooks, trainer materials	10/14/2008	14	1	9/29/2008	9/30/2008	#NAME?	#NAME?	SK	
B1013C	Finance	Communication skills	Ship flips and materials to customer	10/14/2008	13	1	11/13/2004	10/1/2008	#NAME?	#NAME?	SK	
B1013C	Finance	Communication skills	Confirm receipt of materials by customer	10/14/2008	8	1	10/5/2008	10/6/2008	#NAME?		SK	
B1013C	Finance	Communication skills	Send final materials to trainer (trainer sheet, directions)	10/14/2008	3	1	10/10/2008	10/11/2008	#NAME?		SK	
B1013C	Finance	Communication skills	Teach Workshop	10/14/2008	-1	1	10/14/2008	10/15/2008	#NAME?		TR	
B1013C	Finance	Communication skills	Process evals/send to customer (with roster) & trainer	10/14/2008	-7	1	10/20/2008	10/21/2008	#NAME?		SK	

Compiler / Training Design / Workshop with Prework / Sheet1 / Sheet2 / Sheet3

	Project	Task	D-Day	D Minus (End no later than (days))	Time Reqd (days)	Start Date	Due Date	RTT Week Start	RTT Week Due	1st Owner	Status/ Notes
1								#NAME?			
40	Communication skills	Unpack class materials/clean up flips/store	10/14/2008	-7	1	10/20/2008	10/21/2008		#NAME?	SK	
41	Communication skills	Email reinforcement msg #1	10/14/2008	-7	1	10/20/2008	10/21/2008	#NAME?	#NAME?	SK	
42	Communication skills	Email reinforcement msg #2	10/14/2008	-21	1	11/3/2008	11/4/2008	#NAME?	#NAME?	SK	
43	Communication skills	Email reinforcement msg #3	10/14/2008	-35	1	11/17/2008	11/18/2008	#NAME?	#NAME?	SK	
44	Communication skills	Email reinforcement msg #4	10/14/2008	-49	1	12/1/2008	12/2/2008	#NAME?	#NAME?	SK	
45	Communication skills	Prepare final impact report	10/14/2008	-58	1	12/10/2008	12/11/2008	#NAME?	#NAME?	CO	
46	Project Mgmt	Check inventory of all materials (books, instruments, etc.)	10/30/2007	21	1	10/8/2007	10/9/2007	#NAME?	#NAME?	SK	
47	Project Mgmt	Make flip charts	10/30/2007	21	2	10/7/2007	10/9/2007		#NAME?	SK	
48	Project Mgmt	Make edits to course materials	10/30/2007	21	4	10/5/2007	10/9/2007	#NAME?	#NAME?	CO	
49	Project Mgmt	Confirm final number of materials needed.	10/30/2007	20	1	10/9/2007	10/10/2007	#NAME?	#NAME?	CO	
50	Project Mgmt	Final proof pre-production	10/30/2007	19	1	10/10/2007	10/11/2007	#NAME?	#NAME?	SK	
51	Project Mgmt	Prepare Master(s) for Kinkos (including covers); verify you have NEWEST version; take to Kinkos	10/30/2007	18	1	10/11/2007	10/12/2007	#NAME?	#NAME?	SK	
52	Project Mgmt	Schedule trainer travel; File travel itinerary.	10/30/2007	16	1	10/13/2007	10/14/2007	#NAME?	#NAME?	TR	
53	Project Mgmt	Materials due back from Kinkos	10/30/2007	16	0	10/14/2007	10/14/2007	#NAME?	#NAME?		
54	Project Mgmt	Proof materials post production/assemble binders	10/30/2007	15	1	10/14/2007	10/15/2007	#NAME?	#NAME?	SK	
55	Project Mgmt	Send room set up and equipment needs to Cust. (write up instructions for Cust.)	10/30/2007	14	1	10/15/2007	10/16/2007	#NAME?	#NAME?	SK	
56	Project Mgmt	Pack workbooks, trainer materials & toys; proof	10/30/2007	14	1	10/15/2007	10/16/2007	#NAME?	#NAME?	SK	
57	Project Mgmt	Ship flips and materials to customer	10/30/2007	13	1	11/13/2004	10/17/2007	#NAME?	#NAME?	SK	
58	Project Mgmt	Process surveys	10/30/2007	9	2	10/19/2007	10/21/2007	#NAME?	#NAME?	SK	
59	Project Mgmt	Confirm receipt of materials by customer	10/30/2007	8	1	10/21/2007	10/22/2007	#NAME?	#NAME?	SK	
60	Project Mgmt	Proof survey reports.	10/30/2007	8	1	10/21/2007	10/22/2007	#NAME?	#NAME?	SK	
61	Project Mgmt	Make final edits to survey reports.	10/30/2007	7	1	10/22/2007	10/23/2007	#NAME?	#NAME?	SK	
62	Project Mgmt	Prepare surveys for shipping	10/30/2007	4	1	10/25/2007	10/26/2007	#NAME?	#NAME?	SK	
63	Project Mgmt	Send final materials to trainer (trainer sheet, directions, survey)	10/30/2007	3	1	10/26/2007	10/27/2007	#NAME?	#NAME?	SK	
64	Project Mgmt	Teach Workshop	10/30/2007	-1	1	10/30/2007	10/31/2007	#NAME?	#NAME?	TR	
65	Project Mgmt	Prepare invoice; log on Project Schedule; update project schedule.	10/30/2007	-7	1	11/5/2007	11/6/2007	#NAME?	#NAME?	NC	
66	Project Mgmt	Process evals/send to customer (with roster) & trnr, file 1 set in folder	10/30/2007	-7	1	11/5/2007	11/6/2007	#NAME?	#NAME?	SK	
67	Project Mgmt	Unpack class materials/clean up flips/store	10/30/2007	-7	1	11/5/2007	11/6/2007	#NAME?	#NAME?	SK	
68	Project Mgmt	Email follow up msg #1	10/30/2007	-7	1	11/5/2007	11/6/2007	#NAME?	#NAME?	SK	
69	Project Mgmt	Follow up message #2	10/30/2007	-21	1	11/19/2007	11/20/2007	#NAME?	#NAME?	SK	
70	Project Mgmt	Follow up message #3	10/30/2007	-35	1	12/3/2007	12/4/2007	#NAME?	#NAME?	SK	
71	Project Mgmt	Follow up message #4 & FU survey	10/30/2007	-49	1	12/17/2007	12/18/2007	#NAME?	#NAME?	SK	
72	Project Mgmt	Process follow up surveys	10/30/2007	-57	1	12/25/2007	12/26/2007	#NAME?	#NAME?	SK	
73	Project Mgmt	Track survey returns; address errors and solicit missing surveys.	10/30/2007	14	14			#NAME?	#NAME?	SK	

Chapter 2 Wrap-Up

In working through the design phase, and moving forward to development, remember that formative evaluation can start very early in the ADDIE process. Begin checking assumptions and preliminary ideas now: It will save time and trouble later. L. Dee Fink, in Tool 36, asks us to step back and view our preliminary plans with a critical eye and reminds us that laying an effective foundation in the early stages of a project supports a development of a better product later. This chapter concludes with suggestions for dealing with a challenge most trainers and designers face sooner or later: working collaboratively with a subject-matter expert.

Tool 36. Fink's Principles of Good Course Design

Contributed by L. Dee Fink, Ph.D.

Once the general instructional plan is created, go back and review. Does it meet the criteria for a "good course" as outlined by contributor Dee Fink?

A "good course". . .

1. **Challenges learners to HIGHER-LEVEL LEARNING.** All training requires some "lower-level" learning, that is, comprehending and remembering basic information and concepts. But many programs never go beyond this. Examples of "higher-level learning" include problem solving, decision making, critical thinking, and creative thinking.

2. **Uses ACTIVE FORMS OF LEARNING.** Some learning will be "passive," that is, reading and listening. But higher-level learning, almost by definition, requires active learning. One learns to solve problems by solving problems; one learns to think critically by thinking critically; etc.

3. **Gives FREQUENT and TIMELY FEEDBACK to learners on the quality of their learning.** Higher-level learning and active learning require frequent and timely feedback for learners to know whether they are "doing" it correctly. "Frequent" means hourly, daily, or weekly; feedback consisting of "a final quiz" is not sufficient. "Timely" means during the same class if possible, or at the next class session.

4. **Uses a STRUCTURED SEQUENCE OF DIFFERENT LEARNING ACTIVITIES.** Any course needs a variety of forms of learning (e.g., lectures, discussions, small groups, writing), to support both different kinds of learning goals and different learning styles. But these various learning activities also need to be structured in a sequence such that earlier content lays the foundation for complex and higher-level learning tasks later.

Tips for Working with Subject-Matter Experts (SMEs)

Contributed by Jennifer Hofmann, Nanette Miner, Jane Bozarth, and Patti Shank

1. **Get the right SME.** The best SME is not necessarily the one who has been doing the job the longest, but may often be among those who are newer. The newer person is more likely to remember what it was like to not know how to perform the job and can help you identify the information most critical to learner success.

2. **Begin with the end in mind.** Remember what you are trying to accomplish. The SME has expertise you need, so cultivate the relationship that will help you get the results you are after.

3. **Do your homework.** Spend some time researching and reading up on the topic before meeting with the SME. This will gain you respect, increase your credibility, and save the SME time in walking you through basic information.

4. **Remember, the SME already has a job.** Do not ask for unnecessary meetings or extra work on the SME's part. Stay on task in meetings and during interviews. Also make reasonable requests: don't ask the SME to write, for instance, lesson plans or training materials.

5. **Reciprocate.** Give something back. Offer a work/life balance or stress management workshop free for the SME's work unit, or help design the PowerPoint show for the SME's next meeting presentation.

6. **Take responsibility and be proactive.** Provide reasonable deadlines and follow up on agreements; don't wait for the SME to bring material to you. Do not ask the SME to review information that's already been approved.

7. **Ask the right questions.** Ask an SME, "Does the learner need to know this?" and the answer will always be "Yes!" Instead, try asking, "Can you give an example of when the learner would use this information?," or "What is the consequence if the learner does not know this information?"

8. **Thank the SME.** A nice note, or an email copied to the SME's boss, will go a long way toward building goodwill and getting you help next time.

Additional Suggested Resources

Novice test writers often find that creating good tests is far more difficult than it looks. Many universities offer online guidance and tutorials for faculty; search www.google.com for "creating test items" and "writing good tests." Better yet: hire a psychometrist to help you develop valid, reliable, useful tests. For reflective comments on the issue of testing in general, try Roger Schank's *Lessons in Learning, e-Learning, and Training* (Pfeiffer, 2005) Those new to technology-based training will find Thomas Toth's *Technology for Trainers* (ASTD, 2004) and Patti Shank and Amy Sitze's *Making Sense of Online Learning* (Pfeiffer, 2004) good places to start. If formal project planning interests you, try searching www.google.com for "Project Planning Software." Many products offer live demonstrations and free trial periods.

Develop

e now fill out the bare-bones outlines from the design phase with the activities that will support the learning process. We move from blue-printing to creating products such as instructor guides, visuals, and scripts or storyboards. The development phase is where we make the decisions—about activities, exercises, and approaches—that can make the difference between a ho-hum training session and a "wow" learning experience. Choosing particular strategies, developing detailed lesson plans and instructional materials, and providing train-the-trainer activities can be especially challenging for those who are designing instruction that will be delivered by, or with, other trainers. For those developing e-learning, the basic storyboards developed in the design phase are now fully fleshed out in preparation for the handoff to programmers and graphic artists.

This chapter offers tools and tips for choosing among various instructional strategies, designing effective job aids, tailoring approaches to differing learning styles and preferences, and creating online courses. For those developing training to be delivered by others there are a variety of templates for formatting instructor guides.

In the interest of rapid design, consider piloting items at this stage, rather than waiting until everything is developed, you can get reactions to video clips, smooth the edges of demonstrations, check the display on the PowerPoint shows, test exam items for clarity and bias. Overall: You can take steps now to help determine whether this plan will likely get you the results you are after.

Instructional Methods: Basics

This section includes some guidelines for choosing and using instructional methods. The first is a quick overview chart; the others offer more detailed advice about popular methods such as lectures, discussions, demonstrations, case studies, and role plays. Several items ask not only whether a particular approach is appropriate, but also assess whether your skills and personality make it an effective approach for you.

Tool 37. Instructional Methods: Advantages and Disadvantages

Contributed by Ann Downer

Method	Advantages	Disadvantages	Comments
		Purpose of Block of Instruction: Informational	
Lecture; **Lecturette (shorter);** **Lecture forum** (with question cards or question/answer period).	Transmits lots of information. Lecturette shorter. Efficiently facilitated forum allows exploration of content in more detail.	Audience is a largely passive role. Communication one-way.	Trainer should be an interesting speaker, able to self-limit and stick to time, be able to facilitate questions effectively.
Panel; **Panel forum;** **Expanding panel** (vacant chair—individual can join panel when wishing to express opinion).	Adds different points of view to content. Change of speakers can support interest and attention.	Largely passive role of participants with exception of expanding panel; expanding panel not practical with groups larger than twenty.	Can be challenging to facilitate; leader must express solid set of ground rules and skill to enforce them.
Debate	Provides different points of view; thought-provoking.	Largely passive audience.	(same as for panel)
Presentation; **Presentation with listening teams** (participants given listening assignment before presentation; question speaker afterward); **Presentation with reaction panel** (small group listens and forms panel following presentation).	Lots of information; fast; new points of view; a more organized question and answer format; reaction panel can speak.	Audience largely passive; reaction panel may not represent all views of group.	Trainer should structure listening assignment with clear purpose; must select panelists from a cross-section of the group.

From Analysis to Evaluation: Tools, Tips, and Techniques for Trainers.
Copyright © 2008 by John Wiley & Sons, Inc. Reproduced by permission of Pfeiffer, an Imprint of Wiley. www.pfeiffer.com

Method	Advantages	Disadvantages	Comments
Videotape or DVD; Slides; Educational TV	Reinforce content, add entertainment; can help to focus attention; can be good for sparking discussion; flexible start and stop for discussion	Passive methods for an audience; possibility of equipment problems; can be overused	Short, especially relevant or provocative video clip can provide good opener; where appropriate introduce by telling learners what to notice: say, "Look for ____, ____, and." Prior to session load video, cue up to desired start spot, and check volume for playback
Group discussion (of given topic); **Buzz groups** (short, time-limited discussion on given subject).	Participants are active; allows chance to hear other points of view; quieter people can express themselves. Pools collective knowledge of groups;	Discussions can easily go off track; strong personalities can dominate; inexperienced leader may have difficulty facilitating effectively; can be time-consuming	Trainer should be able to give clear instructions and keep discussion on target. Groups of four to six most effective. Important for trainer to help keep discussions on track and bring to conclusion on time.
Brainstorming. Part 1: Quick all-learners activity in which learners are presented with problem or issue and work to quickly generate as many ideas or solutions as possible. Part 2: Facilitator guides exploration and evaluation of ideas generated in Part 1.	Good for problem solving; quick change of pace; allowing all to participate; validates ideas of group.	Needs clear trigger question and evaluation/ discussion following; requires careful facilitation in order to maintain focus on generating quantity, rather than evaluation, of ideas.	Do not evaluate, criticize, omit, or discuss contributions until all are written; record in contributor's own words; use another person to record if possible.
Reading (alone or aloud); Reading with discussion or report.	More actively involving (as opposed to trainer reading material or reviewing text content on PowerPoint slides); provides a chance for in-depth insight and different perspectives.	May require more reading/ writing skills than participants have; leader may have to fill in after reports.	Requires skill to select relevant material; learners need reading skills. Ask for volunteers for read-aloud assignments to avoid embarrassing those with weak reading skills.

Purpose of Block of Instruction: Attitudinal Change

Role Play. Participants enact different roles in applying skills learned in training to analyzing or solving a problem. See Tool 42. Using a Role Play.	Useful for practice of new skills, active for participants and observers can impact attitude and behavior; can be powerful learning in placing learners into "another's shoes"	Requires maturity and willingness of groups; requires excellent facilitation skills of trainer. Must be relevant to learner's real work life.	Trainer needs skill and understanding; getting people into roles, giving directions, establishing climate of trust. Trainer needs insight into threat posed by activity to some individuals; ability to help group process and debrief. Use in well-formed group. Can be structured into dyad, triad, and fishbowl.
Simulations. More elaborate than a case study, simulations place the learner is placed into a complex "real" situation. For example, the learners working for a social services agency is put through a replication of the process for applying for public assistance. Sometimes sold as packaged products.	Intense involvement skills practice in problem solving and decision-making; competitive.	Competitive; requires a game and possibly consultant to help facilitate; time-consuming. May require multiple players so can be difficult to staff.	Requires leader preparation to familiarize with rules and directions.
Task groups. Different small groups assigned specific and different tasks to work on or problems to solve	Sustained interaction allows quieter people to express themselves; validates participants.	Time-consuming; requires great degree of self-direction and group maturity.	Keep groups small and diverse with sustained interaction and clear purpose.

Method	Advantages	Disadvantages	Comments
Purpose of Block of Instruction: Behavioral Change			
Role Play. Participants enact different roles in applying skills learned in training to analyzing or solving a problem. (See Tool 42, Using a Role Play.)	Useful for practice of new skills, active for participants and observers can impact attitude and behavior.	Requires maturity and willingness of groups; requires excellent facilitation skills of trainer.	Trainer needs skill and understanding; getting people into roles, giving directions, establishing climate of trust. Trainer needs insight into threat posed by activity to some individuals; ability to help group process and debrief. Use in well-formed group. Can be structured into dyad, triad, and fishbowl.
Simulation. More elaborate than a case study, simulations place the learner into a complex "real" situation. For example, during training on new project management software, learners are provided with detailed information about an elaborate hypothetical project and asked to develop a plan for completing it. Sometimes sold as prepackaged products.	Intense involvement skills practice in problem solving and decision making; competitive.	Competitive; requires a game and possibly consultant to help facilitate; time-consuming. May require multiple players so can be difficult to staff.	Requires leader preparation to familiarize with rules and directions.
Audio recording with playback; Video recording with playback	Very concrete learning tool; participant involved in judging own performance.	Criteria must be clear; feedback and assessment based on specific behaviors; requires equipment.	Trainer should establish purpose and performance criteria clearly. Technique can be threatening; ensure safe environment for learners.
Case study. (See Tool 41. Using a Case Study.)	Opportunity to apply new knowledge; requires judgment good assessment tool; participant active; chance to practice skills.	Case study must be relevant to learner's needs and daily concerns.	Trainer needs to have knowledge and skills sufficient to "solve" the problem; may need to design own studies; compare approaches of several groups and reinforce best solutions.

Method			
"In-basket" (form of case study or simulation). Learners are given all materials relevant to a situation and asked to apply skills to resolving or solving it. For example, a learner in a training class on delegation skills for new supervisors is given materials associated with a typical work day, such as letters, memos, email, phone messages, and notes about typical daily interactions, and asked to prioritize and delegate tasks.	Helps participant to clarify and crystallize thoughts, opinions, values; opportunity to apply knowledge to "real" situation.	Must be relevant assignment to participant; may require strong reading and/or writing skills.	Leader needs knowledge of participant's daily concerns/needs; ability to critique responses.
Demonstration; Demonstration with practice (by participants).	Allows for optional modeling of desired behavior/skill can be active; good for learning simple skills.	Method more effective if participants are active; feedback must follow immediately after practice.	Requires skill to model desired behavior; break procedure down into simple steps; ability to provide feedback.
Skills practice lab (small participant groups practice together)	Different points of view and feedback; participant active; good for translating information into skills.	Group should have enough knowledge or insight to coach one another.	Act as a resource to groups.
Purpose of Block of Instruction: Planning			
Group discussion with decision-making regarding a new action; Individual or group planning session with report	Validates maturity and needs of group members; members have best insight into own problems and needs on-the-job; group leaves session with practical, constructive and mutual goals; groups get ideas from one another.	Requires mature group that can self-direct and stay on task; time-consuming.	Leader should serve as resource once directions are given.

Tool 38. Choosing a Lecture

Contributed by Honolulu Community College Faculty Development

*The purpose of a lecture is to **clarify** information to a large group in a short period of time. It is not just to transmit content. (I once attended a conference at which performance-based training specialist Sivasailam Thiagarajan, aka "Thiagi," defined "transfer of learning" as "transferring information from the instructor's mouth to the learner's note pad without anything ever passing through a human brain.") It is an instructor-centered strategy and largely viewed as a way for trainers to feed their own egos. And, while it seems everyone agrees that lecture is not a very effective approach, it is still widely used, most recently taking the form of the PowerPoint-as-teleprompter approach to delivering content.*

The following questions should assist you in helping you think through whether a lecture is the most appropriate strategy to use, whether it is the best approach for the given content, and whether it fits your abilities and preferences. Among other things, the questions urge you to honestly assess whether you are tempted to lecture to suit your own ego needs when another approach would do. As you read through these, consider the lecture from the learner's point of view.

1. What knowledge, skill, or attitude needs to be learned? Is lecture the best way to facilitate that learning?

2. Do all or most of the learners need the content now? Could it be provided as written or online pre-work?

3. How much preparation time is available? Do you have time to draft and rehearse the lecture, and create or locate good visuals and other supporting materials?

4. Can you make the lecture interesting and compelling?

5. Would a handout work just as well?

6. Can you devise means to ensure that more than one sense is used by learners? How can you provide them with the opportunity to do more than just listen? Can you provide, for instance, an outline for note-taking?

7. Are there natural divisions in material that equate to 15 minutes or less?

8. Would a video clip work just as well?

9. Do your impromptu lectures last 5 minutes or less?

10. Could you provide an outline of important parts of the lecture?

11. What portion of your total teaching time do you spend lecturing?

12. Do you summarize regularly in the lecture?

13. Do you pose questions in your lectures? Are learners given some opportunity to interact with you during the lecture?

14. Have you ever listened to or watched one of your lectures? Are you interesting, engaging, and articulate?

Tool 39. Choosing a Demonstration

Contributed by Honolulu Community College Faculty Development

The purpose of the demonstration is to transmit the big picture to a relatively small group of learners in a short period of time. Demonstrations usually require a lot of preparation time and must be supported with the materials actually used in carrying out the task. Demonstrations are particularly useful in teaching physical skills but are more trainer-centered than learner-centered.

In thinking about using a demonstration, give some consideration to the factors below regarding the appropriateness of the approach, the constraints that you will face, and issues (such as whether you will take questions during the activity) that will help you prepare to conduct the demonstration.

1. Does the learner need to see the process?

2. Can you tell and show the content?

3. Do you want the learners to imitate you? (This may require multiple work stations and sets of materials.)

4. Could you use a video just as well?

5. Can the learners take notes?

6. Will there be practice time for the learners?

7. Can the learner easily identify the steps they are viewing? (A demonstration held before a large audience in a large room may be hard for all to see.)

8. Is there only one right way? Will you demonstrate alternatives?

9. Will you support the demonstration with handouts?

10. Have you ever listened to or watched one of your demonstrations? Are you interesting, engaging, and articulate? Are you good at giving instructions?

Tool 40. Choosing a Discussion

Contributed by Honolulu Community College Faculty Development

The purpose of a discussion is to solicit and involve the learners in the training experience. As discussion promotes understanding and clarification of concepts, ideas, and feelings, it can be a very useful technique with content aimed at attitude change. There are numerous variations, and the discussion method can vary from trainer-centered to learner-centered. Role playing, debate, panel discussion, reviews, supervised study, brainstorming, buzz groups, idea incubation, tests, show-and-tell, worksheets, conferences, and interviews are examples. Creating circumstances such that learners can interact with one another—rather than just participate in a back-and-forth conversation with the trainer—is additionally challenging as it requires the relinquishing of some control by the trainer, and as a rule requires the creation of small groups (eight or fewer learners).

The following questions ask you to consider the opportunities and constraints inherent to a discussion activity in determining whether it will be appropriate for your purposes.

1. Do you need active involvement from the learner?

2. Must you (the trainer) hear everything being said? You will not be able to monitor every word of simultaneous discussions.

3. How much time is available? Discussions take time and learners should not feel rushed.

4. Is divergent thinking a desirable end? Can there be more than one right answer?

5. Could you just as well tell them? What do you hope will be gained by discussion?

6. Is there time to clarify differences that arise during discussions?

7. How much control do you feel you need? You will not be able to control every facet of multiple simultaneous discussions.

8. Can you accept the learners' views?

9. Can interest be aroused and maintained? Is the topic interesting?

10. Is there time to draw conclusions?

11. Is there time to follow up?

12. Why is two-way communication important in this situation?

13. Are checks and balances available to prevent certain learners from dominating the discussion?

14. Have you ever listened to or watched yourself in a discussion? Using discussion effectively requires a flexible, facilitative training style.

Instructional Methods: Advanced Techniques

While techniques such as discussions and demonstrations are fairly straightforward, other techniques may require more in the way of preparation and in-class facilitation. This section includes tools for effectively using case studies, role plays, and stories to support training and encourage participant interaction with material and each other.

Tool 41. Using a Case Study

Contributed by Shawn Scheffler

Choosing a Case Study

A case study is used to allow participants to analyze or synthesize a situation and apply principles to solving problems. It is, essentially, a description of an incident that involves a problem and a necessary decision.

Writing Case Studies

The case can be real or fabricated. When descriptions of actual cases are used, the actual solution or decision can be presented at the end of the analysis. Case studies consist of a case report, analysis, and discussion. It may precede, follow, or take the place of content presentation.

The Case Report—Describes a Situation That Has Reached a Climax

- Provide a realistic situation, one that has happened or will likely happen.

- Describe the evolution and/or history of the incident.

- Choose a concept that is applicable to as many participants as possible.

- Indicate all relevant detail

- Displays may be textual descriptions, audio/video examples, or acted out by the facilitator.

The Case Analysis—A Guided Discussion of the Situation

- Organize the analysis with a set of questions. Examples: What are the key issues? What created this problem? What larger problem could this be a symptom for? What are some reasons? What conditions contributed? What went wrong? What action should have been taken? What will the consequences be? What are the responsibilities of each party?

- Give the participants clear directions regarding time constraints and the expected product or results.

- Place the analysis in an open group (all participants) or in small groups.

- Direct individuals to write down their own ideas before working in the group.

The Case Discussion—The Sharing of Participant Solutions or Ideas

- Anticipate possible solutions and discussion points.

- Facilitate discussion to connect the results with the lesson.

Approaches to Case Studies

- Ask individual learners to describe a situation, then swap with another learner

- Provide learners with a prepared problem to analyze

- Provide learners with an overview of a critical incident

Individual	Problem Analysis	Critical Incident
1. Each learner develops a short narrative describing a past situation.	1. Learners exchange case information.	1. Each person analyzes the partner's case and reports back.
2. Learners are given a prepared case study.	2. Each individual or group sorts the information, discusses the problem, and attempts to identify a solution.	2. Learners report the findings and discuss the results.
3. The incident is described, but all information is not provided.	3. Learners ask questions to bring relevant information to light and reconstruct the situation.	3. Case analysis occurs and decisions are presented.

Note: When developing case studies, don't provide extraneous detail or irrelevant facts that may sidetrack the solution. Our aim is to reinforce a process, not confuse the learner. Generally, case studies will be two or three paragraphs in length—no more than one page.

Tool 42. Using a Role Play

Contributed by Shawn Scheffler

A good role play experience creates powerful learning, but requires thoughtful preparation and a very skilled facilitator. It can also be very threatening to learners. One great piece of advice here, from contributor Shawn Scheffler: "Call it something else."

Why Use a Role Play?

- To model the actual task or interaction

- To test the higher levels of Bloom's taxonomy: analysis, synthesis, evaluation

- To create personal awareness of a skill gap

- To identify areas for improvement

Developing Successful Role Plays

1. Match the exercise to the instruction.

Relevance	Test a major objective or perform a substantial task
Style	Do not use a "fun" activity with a serious subject.
Timing	No single exercise should comprise more than 10 percent of the total training time.
Complexity	Refrain from adding extraneous data and overly difficult tasks.
Group size	Consider the effects of audience size on directing, monitoring, and debriefing a given number of participants.

2. Choose a format appropriate to the instruction, the topic, the desired outcome, and, where possible, realistic workplace performance. Examples are offered in italics.

Informal	Takes place spontaneously, no written material or preplanning.
	Customer service rep answers telephone call from angry customer.
Acted out	Demonstrated by the trainer to illustrate a point.
	Trainer plays the role of convicted child molester to demonstrate techniques used to lure a child into a car.
Observed	Includes multiple positions, typically two players and an observer.
	Show exemplar of performance appraisal discussion.

Reversal	Players complete the exercise and switch roles.
	Learners assume roles of different genders, minorities, or professional groups as part of a diversity training program. During the exercise, different participants take turns assuming the same role.
Rotating	Roles shift from player to player.
	During leadership training learners take turns to generate different techniques a manager might use when interacting with a problem performer.
Modeled	Participants conduct the exercise and critique performance. The case study is then reenacted by different participants.
	In a sales technique training session learners watch a possible approach, critique it, then other learners incorporate the critique into a new attempt.
Team-based	Two or more participants represent the two sides and may choose roles within the group.
	Learners in an organizational team-building workshop assume the roles of different, and sometimes conflicting and competing teams, in the organization.

3. Prepare all the necessary details.

- Players/Roles

- Situation

- Problem

- Scripts

- Objectives

4. Call it *something* else.

- Behavior modeling

- Skill practice

- Simulation

- Dialogue

- Interview

Conducting Successful Role Plays

A great deal of a role play's success is based on effective delivery. What we prepare in the participant text will give the framework for the exercise. However, the real "life" of a role play comes from proper delivery, monitoring, and debriefing of the activity.

The four stages of the role play process are described below and shown in Figure 3.1.

1. Introduction—The goals are to get the audience involved, relieve tension, and sell the benefits of completing the activity. Focus on making a connection between the activity and the material covered.

   • Provide an overview of the activity and its objectives.

   • Describe the benefits and value of the exercise.

   • Project enthusiasm and reassurance.

2. Direction—The goal is to guide learners toward a successful experience by providing clear expectations and instructions.

   • Form groups prior to giving instructions; be directive and vary the groups.

   • Assign roles (recorder, timekeeper, leader, etc.) if necessary.

   • Present the big picture, then move sequentially through the desired process.

Figure 3.1. Role-Play Process

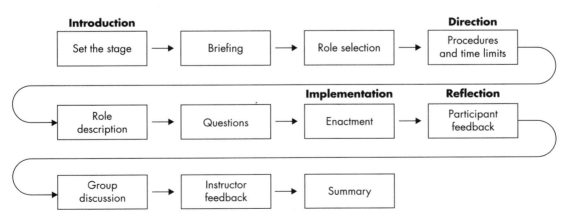

- Break the instructions down into detailed, sequential steps

- Be clear about time, restrictions, and expected results.

- Speak slowly and define terms.

- Walk the group through an example.

- Read narratives aloud.

3. Implementation—The goals are to monitor and manage the activity.

   - Circulate among the groups; monitor for signals of confusion and observe the process.

   - If a group is unproductive, take temporary leadership to get them back on track.

   - If a group moves too quickly, offer a challenge, give additional assignments, or probe to raise other issues.

   - Help the groups keep time; give "minute warnings" or a countdown.

4. Reflection—The goal is to process the meaning and value of the activity.

   - Obtain learners' feedback and opinions before offering your own.

   - Prepare two to four questions that are related to the activity's objectives.

   - When groups are reporting back, set time parameters and make notes on a flip chart or chalkboard.

   - Obtain reports from all groups before moving to general discussion.

Role Play Structure

In a given role-play scenario characters may enact open or covert roles. An *open* role is one in which all the information about a character is provided: what prompted the interaction, what knowledge the character does or does not have. A *covert* role is one in which a character is in possession of knowledge that is not provided to others participating in the role play. For example: In a supervisory training program the learner playing the role of supervisor may be asked to interact with an "employee" who is voicing valid complaints about an incident involving a co-worker, but

General scenario—open roles	Detailed scenario and characters— open roles	Reenactment of actual situation	Detailed scenario— optional roles	Detailed scenario—covert roles and behavior instructions	Written roles demonstrating specific skills	Roles totally scripted

Unstructured   Structured

cannot divulge the confidential information that the co-worker has already been disciplined for the incident.

Role Considerations

- Open roles may be played immediately upon description of the situation or following a group discussion of how the roles should be played.

- When roles are covert, opportunity should be given for players to get into character and to ask questions. Covert roles are generally revealed during the summary discussion.

- It is helpful to players if roles are written to "you" and if non-gender-specific names are used. (For instance: "You are a customer service representative at a busy call center, and your supervisor, Chris, has just asked to see you about a complaint.")

A Role Aid

This job aid can be used as a quick reminder of the major steps involved in placing, designing, and conducting a role play.

Filter 1

All topics/objectives/
information

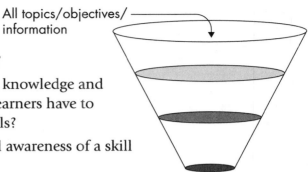

- Does the task require practice of this nature?
- Does it test more than knowledge and comprehension? Do learners have to apply and practice skills?
- Does it create personal awareness of a skill gap?

Filter 2

- Does it match the type of instruction and audience (style, timing, complexity, group size)?
- Is it the proper format (acted out, observed, reversal, rotating, modeled, team-based)?

Filter 3

- Have I prepared all the necessary details to describe the role play?
- Have I called it something besides a "role play"?

Tool 43. Getting the Most from the Stories You Use

Contributed by Lori Silverman

Need to capture people's attention? Get a point to stick with them? Or communicate a difficult concept? Try using stories. While trainers often tell stories spontaneously, to obtain maximum results, take the time to select those stories you would like to use in advance of sharing them and to deliberately think about where they fit best into your training plan.

Selecting a Story

Here are five criteria for selecting stories to use in training.

- **Who** will hear your story/stories? Know your learners' background and demographics. Ensure the story and its wording are appropriate for them so you do not inadvertently offend someone.

- **What** learning objective are you are trying to achieve? The story needs to fulfill it. While a story may not strictly "fit" the topic (for example, metaphorical or symbolic stories or one about an experience you had as a child), the key point of the story should match the objective for which it is being used. In addition, recognize that individual stories have their own purposes, such as evoking reactions around a topic, deepening learning around a specific point, and pointing out the difference between appropriate and inappropriate behaviors.

- **Where** will you physically be telling the story? Know the room and where it is located—and who else may inadvertently hear the stories. Not all building walls are soundproof.

- **When** will you tell a story relative to other information that you will share? Avoid painful or embarrassing stories or those that speak to life-and-death challenges until you have established rapport and credibility. Consider using stories as case studies in addition to sharing them orally.

- **How** will you be perceived, given the story/stories you share? Perception is everything. Learners will learn a lot about you, even if you use stories that are not your own. While personal stories are easier to tell because you can recall the experience, be aware that you may be labeled as self-centered and arrogant if you only share your own.

Using Stories

Be creative. There are many ways to use stories in training. Ideally, the best time to think about where to use stories is immediately after you have created a skills hierarchy when you are determining what training methods to use. Here are some rules of thumb to help you.

- If you sense people may be tired or distracted, open a topic with a story to capture their attention.

- If you suspect learners may resist what you have to share, relay a story beforehand that helps them understand its importance.

- If you are unsure that learners will be able to easily comprehend data you have to communicate, tell a story afterward that brings meaning to it—or tell one early on that leads into the need for the findings.

- If you feel learners need more details around how to use a specific skill or how to employ the theory or model behind it, use a story that elaborates on what you have shared.

- If you want learners to see the impact (or potential outcome) of particular behaviors, provide a success story or one that speaks to the consequences of inappropriate actions.

- If you know from experience that learners are going to ask certain questions, prepare stories to answer them as they arise.

- If you are skeptical that people will do what has been asked of them or you want to reinforce content, follow up with a story that speaks to the need to take action.

Content adapted by Lori Silverman from Silverman, L. "Timeless Tips for Telling Stories." *Communication World Bulletin*, December 2006.

Tool 44. The Job Aid Job Aid

Contributed by Patti Shank

A special challenge in the design phase is differentiating what learners need to memorize versus what they need to find. Good job aids are concise references that support and guide performance. Here's a great job aid for creating a job aid—hence, the name.

When to Use a Job Aid

Job aids are useful for supporting and guiding performance when the ability to self-correct is needed and the task:

- Is performed infrequently (so the performer is unlikely to remember what to do),

- Is straightforward (so the task can be described concisely),

- Relies on facts that aren't easily remembered or that change frequently, and/or

- Doesn't require great speed (so the performer has time to *use* a job aid).

Job aids are also useful when training time or availability is limited but performance help is needed. Job aids can be useful alongside or instead of training.

Benefits of Job Aids

Potential benefits of job aids include:

- Reduced cost and time (compared to training)

- Less reliance on performer memory (which is limited)

- Improved transfer of instruction to the workplace (the goal of workplace instruction)

- More consistent performance

- Reduction in performance errors

Sections

Most job aids are broken into sections that can be easily scanned by the user. Clear headings and bulleted text can be helpful. The formatting of this tool is an example.

Types

The table below describes three types of job aids, elements that are typically included in each type of job aid, and some examples of each type of job aid.

Job Aid Type	Typical Information Formats Included	Examples
Informational. Definitions and facts	Logically organized data table or list	Phone book, zip codes by county, lab tests/ costs, intellectual property terminology
Procedural. How-tos	Step table, outline, checklist, flow chart	Gift returns, travel reimbursements, entering an exception, out-of-network billing, making a table of contents from headings codes
Analytical. What to consider	Checklist, decision table, worksheet	Interview hints, troubleshooting your digital camera, selecting a wedding venue, which cold medicine is right for you, smoking cessation options

Job aids should be concise and short. It is acceptable to combine types in one job aid, but if the job aid starts getting long or meandering, consider breaking the job aid into separate job aids. For example, a Return Codes (informational) job aid and a Return Process (procedural) job aid.

Steps for Creating a Job Aid

1. Determine what performers need to be able to do.

2. Determine whether job aids are appropriate, and which type(s) and element(s) are needed.

3. Write content (with proficient performer assistance). *Fine-tune for brevity and clarity.*

4. Pilot and observe use. Tweak. Tweak again as needed.

Information Formats

The following table lists common information formats that are used in job aides, some crucial considerations when using the element, and an example of each type of element.

Element	Crucial Considerations	Example
Data table	Logical order (typically chronological or alphabetical); easy to skim	
Diagram or chart	Easy to distinguish components; callouts or legend needed?	
Flow chart	Easy to follow; legend (meaning of shapes or colors) needed?	
Step table	Logical order by step number; important to spell out expected result?	

For the Data table example:

Department	Floor
Advertising	3
Editorial	1

For the Step table example:

Step	Action	Result
3.	Select name	Personal record appears
4.	Select account	Selected account appears

Element	Crucial Considerations	Example		
Decision table	Limited options (or too hard to use)	**Result Code**	**Action**	
		1–224 (a–g)	ring sale	
		1–224 (h–z)	request ID	
		2–225 (ALL)	transfer to supervisor	

Examples

The following URLs provide examples of real job aids. Notice whether they are well formatted and concise.

www.aim.fsu.edu/job_aids/deprep.htm

www.cu.edu/System_Controller/fin-system-job-aids.html

www.southalabama.edu/petal/jobaids.htm

For More Information

Rossett, A., & Gautier-Downes, J. (1991). *A handbook of job aids.* San Francisco, CA: Pfeiffer.

Rossett, A., & Schaffer, L. (2007). *Job aids and performance support: Moving from knowledge in the classroom to knowledge anywhere.* San Francisco, CA: Pfeiffer.

Matching Methods to Learning Styles and Preferences

The idea of learning styles and preferences, first mentioned in Chapter 1: Analyze, is for many designers and trainers an "easier said than done" proposition: It is only natural for us to gravitate toward our own likes and needs (and creating "training" that is little more than a slide-show-supported lecture is dangerously easy, although we know most learners don't learn well by passively listening to an instructor talk). While there are many theories on learning styles, all are based on the idea that different people learn in different ways. It's important for us to "mix it up" in designing instruction and develop flexibility in our classroom skills and own preferences.

The tools in this section offer ideas for activities and approaches relative to several different theories of learning styles and preferences. An important note: The means for addressing the needs of different learning styles and preferences have to be closely tied to the instruction, not offered only as token effort. Many PowerPoint shows used in training, for instance, utilize busy backgrounds and cute, but irrelevant, clip art. This does not help the "visual" learner; rather, it often confuses everyone, detracts from the message, and, according to research,[1] may actually harm the learning experience.

---

[1]Clark, R., Nguyen, R., & Sweller, J. (2005). *Efficiency in learning: Evidence-based guidelines to manage cognitive load.* San Francisco, CA: Pfeiffer.

Tool 45. Activities for Visual, Auditory, and Kinesthetic Preferences

The simplest, and possibly best-known, vision of learning preferences is the VAK (visual-auditory-kinesthetic) model. As I mentioned in Chapter 1, it's not very difficult for most of us to identify our own preferences: Are you a good listener, or an impatient one? Do you like to tinker and put things together? Would you prefer to read a book or listen to that book on a CD? The quick quiz: When you receive a new electronic product, such as an iPod, do you read the manual all the way through, call a friend who has one, or play with it until it works? A word of warning about over-generalizing, though, as one preference can sometimes be another in disguise. I've been in the training business for nearly two decades, with extensive graduate work in training and development, and thought I understood the concept of learning styles inside and out. For years I believed my proclivity for note-taking was evidence of a strong visual learning preference, until a colleague pointed out that I never actually went back and looked at those notes, ever: for me, the writing satisfied a kinesthetic, not a visual, need.

Visual (Seeing, Reading)	Auditory (Listening and Speaking)	Kinesthetic (Touching and Doing)
Posters	Discussions	Role plays
Post-its	Reading aloud	Group activities
PowerPoint slides	Oral quizzes or other challenges	Hands-on activities
Diagrams		Experiential activities
Mind maps	Background music	Opportunities for note-taking—to be in motion
Color-coded materials	Debates	
Videos	Giving reports	Hands-on games/puzzles
Graphics	Storytelling	Lab activities
Flow charts	Verbal instructions	Field trips
Models	Verbal games/ puzzles	Games
Written instructions	Opportunities for verbal review of material	Building something
Opportunities for note-taking—to review notes later	Paired work	
Journaling, blogging	Interviewing	
Visual games/puzzles	Verbal brainstorming	
Written brainstorming		

Tool 46: Multiple Intelligences Activities

Contributed by Lenn Millbower

Based on Gardner's theory of multiple intelligences, more in-depth than the VAK model discussed in Tool 45, this chart is a guide for designing learning program activities.

Bodily/Kinesthetic	*Musical/Rhythmic*
❑ Acting	❑ Analyzing lyrics
❑ Hand-eye coordination	❑ Listening to music
❑ Manipulating objects	❑ Reciting rhymes
❑ Movement	❑ Singing
❑ Playing sports	❑ Tapping rhythms
❑ Gesturing	❑ Writing songs
Intrapersonal	*Naturalist*
❑ Goal setting	❑ Categorizing items
❑ Individual study	❑ Exploring natural patterns
❑ Introspection	❑ Growing plants
❑ Journaling	❑ Hiking or walking
❑ Solo tasks	❑ Observing animals
❑ Visualizing memories	❑ Studying outdoors
Interpersonal	*Verbal/Linguistic*
❑ Group sharing	❑ Group discussions
❑ Interactive games	❑ Oral presentations
❑ Open discussion	❑ Reading quotes
❑ Study groups	❑ Storytelling
❑ Teaching others	❑ Word games
❑ Team learning	❑ Writing

Logical/Mathematical	Visual/Spatial
❏ Arranging sequences	❏ Building models
❏ Case studies	❏ Charting
❏ Classifying items	❏ Drawing
❏ Logic puzzles	❏ Jigsaw puzzles
❏ Problem solving	❏ Mind mapping
❏ Strategy games	❏ Visualizations

Tool 47. Multiple Intelligences Matrix

Contributed by Lenn Millbower

This tool is invaluable to those seeking to address myriad learning styles in their training designs. Contributor Lenn Millbower offers the following comments about the Multiple Intelligences Matrix Tool:

- *It does not guarantee a flawless program. It instead provides a snapshot look at your program so you can make intelligent design decisions.*

- *It does not have a definitive mean score. The 4.0 mean is an arbitrary target. The level of interactivity appropriate for one audience may not be appropriate for another.*

- *It provides an impressive tool you can display for clients to demonstrate your professionalism, attention to detail, and instructional design expertise.*

How to Use the Multiple Intelligences Matrix Tool

Step 1—Dividing your program into 3-minute segments, determine which of the eight intelligences you use in each segment.

Step 2—For each application of Multiple Intelligences (MI), check the corresponding intelligence boxes.

Step 3—Once your analysis is complete, add all of your check marks to determine a total MI score.

Step 4—Divide your MI score by the number of segments in your program.

Step 5—Compare your score to the target mean of 4.0. The closer to 4.0 your final score, the more effectively you have layered MI into your program.

Step 6—Look at the flow of your program and identify blocks of time when some intelligences are overused while others are not used enough and adjust your program accordingly.

Step 7—Re-compute your scores for a final mean average.

Figure 3.2 shows a partial screenshot taken from the full tool, a copy of which is available on the CD.

Figure 3.2. Screenshot from the Multiple Intelligences Matrix

	A	B	C	D	E	F	G	H	I	J	K	L	M	N	O	P	Q	R	S	T	U	V	W	X	Y	Z	AA	AB	AC	AD	AE	AF
1	**Multiple Intelligences Layout Tool**																															
2	Bodily/ Kinesthetic	1																														
3	Intrapersonal	1																														
4	Interpersonal	1																														
5	Logical/ Mathematical	1																														
6	Musical/ Rhythmic	1																														
7	Naturalist	1																														
8	Verbal/ Linguistic	1																														
9	Visual/ Spatial	1																														
10	Step Number:		1	2	3	4	5	6	7	8	9	10	11	12	13	14	15	16	17	18	19	20	21	22	23	24	25	26	27	28	29	30
11	Timeline:		0:00	0:03	0:06	0:09	0:12	0:15	0:18	0:21	0:24	0:27	0:30	0:33	0:36	0:39	0:42	0:45	0:48	0:51	0:54	0:57	1:00	1:03	1:06	1:09	1:12	1:15	1:18	1:21	1:24	1:27
12	**MEAN:**			(Determine mean by adding the number of times a tool is checked and dividing that number by the number of presentation segments)																												

Tool 48. e-Learning Development Techniques: Mix It Up!

This tool, offering suggestions for activities and techniques appropriate to different learning preferences, originally appeared in my first book, e-Learning Solutions on a Shoestring (Pfeiffer, 2005). It is based on Ned Hermann's model of brain dominance. I have a copy of this tool on my office wall and use it more than any other job aid in developing instruction. That book didn't include a CD and many readers have contacted me to ask for a printable version of this tool—so here it is. A good deal here is generalizable to classroom training as well as e-learning.

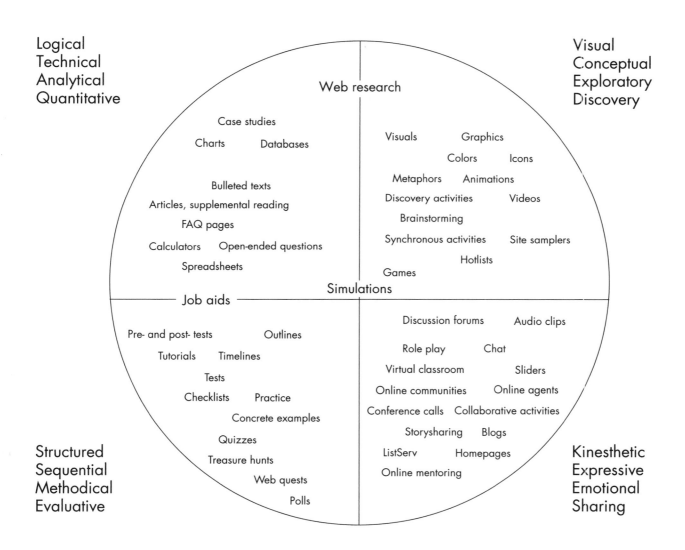

Developing Materials

The development phase of ADDIE is where we create unified packages of materials. Materials must be consistent with one another, useful for the stakeholder for whom they are intended (learner or instructor), and ultimately support the goal of the instruction. This section offers ideas for creating effective handouts for learner use, while Tool 49, Evaluation Worksheet for Graphic Treatment, offers a means of evaluating visual materials with a critical eye. The next section focuses on creating instructor guides for those leading the training.

Tips for Great Handouts

- Leave space for taking notes.

- Don't just provide exact replicas of PowerPoint slides, or if you do, don't put every word of your presentation on the slides.

- Be sure to include instructor or training department contact information.

- Provide suggestions for additional resources and further reading.

- Check your spelling!

- Use headings and white space to help learners access the information.

- Make the handout a valuable tool: include job aids, useful takeaways.

- A good takeaway *supports future use* of the training material.

    - Form follows function. What is the purpose of the handout? If you expect learners to follow along and take notes, use an outline format with plenty of space for writing.

    - If you want participants to have a comprehensive takeaway, provide detailed information and copies of articles and whitepapers.

    - If the handout is to form the basis for in-class discussions, make sure to provide enough data in an accessible format so that learners can quickly read over material and apply it in class.

- Number pages.

- Provide information in memorable ways: checklists, numbered items, meaningful graphics.

- Help learners organize material: provide a matrix, grid, or items showing relationships, such as tables of pros/cons.

- Use themes, such as "journeys" or "mazes."

- Use colors, fonts, white space, and icons to highlight and organize information.

- Remember: Handouts are for the *learner's* use, so design from the learner's point of view.

Tool 49. Evaluation Worksheet for Graphic Treatment

Contributed by Ruth Clark and Chopeta Lyons

It is vital that visual materials support the instructional goals of the training. Too often visual treatments are treated as an afterthought, with a trainer or designer simply picking a preset template to apply to all the slides for a program. Here is a tool from Ruth Clark and Chopeta Lyons, authors of Pfeiffer's excellent Graphics for Learning *(2005).*

1. Generally, does the overall graphic approach support the goal of the training?

    a. What is the goal?

    b. Is the look and feel appropriate to it?

2. Does the overall graphic approach support the context in which the instruction will be used?

    a. Who is the learner?

    b. Does the learner profile include groups that have special visualization attributes, such as color-blindness, different cultural symbols, or difficulty seeing smaller graphics?

    c. What is the learning landscape? Does the environment in which the instruction will be used present any challenges to the learners' ability to see and use the graphics, such as room size, lighting, viewing conditions?

    d. What is the delivery medium?

e. Does the medium present any challenges to displaying the graphics, such as page size, screen resolution, software requirements, or access speed?

3. Does the overall visual approach support the general design needs of the organization and the content?

   a. Does the look and feel project the image or "style" that fits the organization?

   b. Does the look and feel support the instructional strategy?

   c. If the subject matter is "have to show" graphics such as equipment, software screens, or process flows, does the general treatment support their size and layout?

   d. Does the overall visual approach consistently support a graphic or text dominant storyline? And is that choice (graphics or text dominant) appropriate to the content?

   e. Does the general layout of most displays (page or screen) support the desired style, the eye movement (in western cultures, left to right; top to bottom) and orientation of the content graphics?

   f. Do the navigational elements include organizers, such as indicators of where the learners have been, where they are, and where they can go? These may be as simple as topic headers, page number, or paging buttons. Are these in a consistent, but low-impact position within the page or screen?

Developing Instructor Guides

The next items are templates for instructor guides. The challenge in creating a good instructor guide is making it easy for the instructor to follow. If you are the designer, remember that you are closer to the material and the rationale for choosing activities than are the people who will deliver and receive the training. Take a step back and view your completed product from the user's point of view; better yet, pilot the material with potential end-users as you go.

Tool 50. How to Write an Instructor Guide

Contributed by Jean Barbazette

Jean Barbazette has generously provided not only an overview of creating an instructor's guide, but samples of guides for the same topic in three different formats. These are included as Tools 51, 52, and 53.

Purpose of an Instructor Guide

Every instructor guide (or leader's guide) is intended by the course designer to be used by the instructor for these purposes:

- As a guide or blueprint for an instructor to conduct training

- As a means of communicating the instructional strategy from the course designer to the instructor through learning objectives

- As a description or list of learning activities, time frames, and materials required to conduct the training

Contents

Instructor guides will be complete and effective if they contain these ten components:

1. Why and how the course was developed.

2. Summary of target audience for whom the course is intended.

3. Overview of course content.

4. Special information about the course strategy.

5. Instructional objectives (also called behavioral objectives).

6. Specific subject matter (content) to complete activities. The content should be prioritized for flexibility in presentation.

7. Description of learning activities, including practice and evaluation.

8. Recommended time frames for each activity and breaks.

9. Transitions for each activity.

10. Summary of learning points.

Types of Instructor Guides

There are three types of instructor guides a course designer can consider developing. Scripted, outline, and overview instructor guides each contain different amounts of information for the instructor using the plan. Each is defined as follows:

Scripted instructor guide	provides a written narrative for the instructor to use, has complete lectures and answers to activities, provides specific directions for conducting exercises and using visuals and other materials
Outline instructor guide	provides learning objectives, description of activities and notes about content
Overview instructor guide	lists learning objectives and activities with time frames and material required

How to Choose the Right Type of Instructor Guide

The amount of detail to include in a instructor guide depends on the five factors below. Given a specific subject or class, use each of the following questions to rate each point on a four-point scale or as directed for that factor:

1 = significant, 2 = above average, 3 = average, 4 = minimal or none

_____ 1. The subject-matter expertise of the instructor.

_____ 2. The instructor's knowledge of the adult learning process.

_____ 3. The instructor's comfort with facilitating groups.

_____ 4. The instructor's experience in customizing examples, and/or answering questions about how to apply workshop information back on the job.

_____ 5. The need to have the content of the workshop delivered <u>consistently</u> at each presentation. (4 = great need/ requirement, 1 = little need)

Scores of mostly 3s and 4s would indicate a need for a very detailed, scripted instructor guide, while scores of 1s and 2s suggest the appropriateness of an outline or overview format. Question 5 asks whether the training must be absolutely consistent: for instance, in the case of a complex medical procedure, it may be critical that every person providing training do it in exactly the same way. In this case, regardless of the other scores, it would probably be advisable to create a scripted instructor guide.

Tools 51, 52, and 53 provide examples of the three types of instructor guides to show the type of details needed for the instructor to deliver a course effectively.

Tool 51. Sample Scripted Instructor Guide

Contributed by Jean Barbazette

See Tool 50 for more information on developing instructor guides.

"Selection Interviewing" Workshop

Time	Objective/Activity	Reference
	<u>Objective</u>: Give an introduction and set the learning climate by saying: *"Many of us have been doing selection interviewing for years. This unit is designed to provide you with an update and perhaps offer a few new ideas. We encourage you to share your experiences with the group. You can tell us what works and what doesn't. We'll brush up on specific skills and review changes in employment law."*	Visual 1
5	<u>Activity</u>: Review session objectives on page 1. *"Please turn to page 1 and read the objectives listed. As you read, please circle the numbers of the objectives that are of importance to you."*	Page 1, V 2
20	<u>Activity</u>: Complete the survey of current skill level. *"To start, examine your current skill level by completing the survey on page 2. We will use this information to set individualized goals on page 3."* Allow time to complete survey. Ask participants to select three areas for personal development and fill out objectives on page 3. Summarize the objective setting by giving an overview of the workshop: *"At the end of this session, each of you will have the opportunity to practice your interviewing skills on videotape. The items you have selected that need more skill development can be incorporated into your practice session. We will also discuss many of these items during this unit."* <u>Objective</u>: Determine employee selection criteria using existing job descriptions and performance standards.	Page 2, V 3 Page 3
5	<u>Activity</u>: Lecture: Preparing for the Interview. Lecture on the following: **Selection Criteria:** How do you know what to look for? There are a number of tools that already exist within the company that can give you some assistance in these areas. 1. Review Job Descriptions. 2. Review Performance Standards for the position.	

Time	Objective/Activity	Reference
	3. Discuss operations, plans, and upcoming departmental changes with your supervisor (and perhaps subordinates) to ensure that, if the job is growing and/or changing, the person selected has the necessary qualifications and interests to be able to change with it.	
	4. Develop specific selection criteria that will assist you in choosing the best candidate. Begin thinking about questions that will assist you in determining the applicant's suitability (based on your needs). Remember, selection criteria must meet two standards: (1) they must be job-related and (2) they must be a predictor of job performance.	Page 4
15 to 20	<u>Activity</u>: Read and review the job description and case study.	Pages 5, 6, 7

Tool 52. Sample Outline Instructor Guide

Contributed by Jean Barbazette

See Tool 50 for more information on developing instructor guides.

"Selection Interviewing" Workshop

Time	Objective/Activity	Reference
	Objective: Introduction and set the learning climate. For those who have been doing selection interviewing for years, this unit will provide an update, perhaps offer a few new ideas and review changes in employment law. Encourage participants to share their experiences with the group.	Visual 1
5	Activity: Review session objectives on page 1	Page 1, V 2
20	Activity: Ask participants to examine their current skills by completing a survey and setting objectives. Allow time to complete survey. Select three areas for personal development and fill out objectives on page 3. Preview for participants that they will have the opportunity to practice their interviewing skills on videotape. The items they have selected which need more skill development can be incorporated into the practice session. Objective: Determine employee selection criteria using existing job descriptions and performance standards.	Page 2, V 3 Page 3
20	Activity: Lecture: Preparing for the Interview **Selection Criteria:** How do you know what to look for? Use tools that already exist in the company: 1. Review Job Descriptions. 2. Review Performance Standards for the position. 3. Discuss operations, plans, and upcoming departmental changes to ensure that the person selected has the necessary qualifications. 4. Selection criteria must meet two standards: (1) they must be job related and (2) they must be a predictor of job performance.	Page 4

Time	Objective/Activity	Reference
15 to 20	<u>Activity</u>: Read and review the job description and case. Develop and discuss selection criteria for this case in small groups. <u>Objective</u>: Plan effectively for a selection interview through application screening and question preparation.	Pages 5, 6, 7
10	<u>Activity</u>: Application Review: Read through the list of items, "Common Application Problems." Decide which conditions would prevent you from giving the candidate further consideration. Discuss in small groups and report to the large group. <u>Activity</u>: Distribute sample job applications to each group. Discuss the sample applications and identify positive attributes and questionable issues in relation to the information offered by the applications, based on each participant's experience. Use the "Screening Applications Worksheet" to assist the discussion.	Pages 8, 9
10	Have groups designate a spokesperson to report to the large group. Summarize points to remember about screening at the bottom of page 7.	
5	<u>Activity</u>: Ask participants to read information on the types of questions. Discuss comments and/or needs for clarification. Complete the questions on the bottom of page 10 in a large group discussion.	Page 10
5	<u>Activity</u>: Use page 11 to discuss the value of precisely constructed, deliberate, follow-up questions, which can yield important information.	Page 11
15	<u>Activity</u>: Assign two examples to each group of three to discuss. Discuss reports in the large group. See instructor notes for suggested answers. Encourage students to record results on page 12. <u>Objective</u>: Identify legally permissible questions to ask during an employment interview.	Page 12

Tool 53. Sample Overview Instructor Guide

Contributed by Jean Barbazette

See Tool 50 for more information on developing instructor guides.

Workshop: Selection Interviewing (4 hours)

Time	Objective	Method	Job Aid	Job Aid
	At the end of training the participant will be able to:	What TRAINER does:	What PARTICIPANT does:	
15	Identify current skill level and set personal objectives	review objectives	review objectives/complete survey	pages 1 to 3, Visuals 1 to 3
30	Determine appropriate selection criteria	lecture on four criteria	compare criteria to job descriptions, discuss case study	pages 4 to 7
30	Plan for an interview by screening applications	list common problems, hand out sample applications	large group discussion/screen applications in small groups	applications
10	Ask appropriate questions	lead discussion of how to prepare questions	prepare questions	pages 8 and 9
30	Identify legally permissible questions	large group discussion	review list of questions/discuss answers	pages 10 and 11
20	Avoid interviewing dangers	lecture	case study discussion	page 12
15	Make an appropriate decision	direct discussion	review materials on decisions	page 13
90	Summarize concepts to apply on the job	Video participants	role play interview	video

Tool 54. Instructor Guide Template Using Icons

Contributed by Results Through Training (www.RTTWorks.com)

Here is another version of the outline instructor guide format; this one uses icons as visual prompts for instructors. Note that this one also includes space for—and even encourages—the individual trainer to add in personal anecdotes and examples.

(**Note:** Use this space to instruct trainer to set up the learning environment a certain way.)

Section	Time	Support Materials
Introduction	**(# Minutes)** Objective: Confirm objectives; set tone for training; orient participants to class, and facility. Welcome the group. Introduce yourself. Explain course objectives. Conduct icebreaker	
Topic Name	**(# Minutes)** Objective: Summarize objectives for this section. Introduce the topic objectives in the first bullet. Explain more information. Share some personal examples. Write your personal example here: Conduct an activity. Debrief the activity by asking questions such as: Question 1: Question 2: Question 3: Summarize this section by	

Section	Time	Support Materials
	Transition: *"Use this little box to give the trainer actual words to use when transitioning from one section/activity to another. Put in quotes and italicize the text."*	
Topic Name	**(# MINUTES)** Objective: Summarize objectives for this section. Introduce the topic objectives in the first bullet. Explain more information. Share some personal examples. Write your personal example here: Conduct an activity. Debrief the activity by asking questions such as: Question 1: Question 2: Question 3: Summarize this section by:	
Conclusion	**(# Minutes)** Reference the suggested reading list on the last page of the workbook. Ask each person to finish the pages in the Planner. Distribute Session Evaluation.	

Tool 55. Instructor Guide Template: Synchronous Training

Contributed by Jennifer Hofmann and Nanette Miner, Ed.D.

An instructor guide for synchronous training will also have to include instructions for using the tools, such as chat and the whiteboard, and notes for the producer supporting the session. The "Selection" training topic from Jean Barbazette's "How to Write an Instructor Guide" (Tool 50) is used in the completed example below. I like these icons so much that I now use them in developing instructor guides for classroom use.

Throughout the guide you will see icons that will assist you in conducting the class:

?	Prompt to ask for questions.
ⓘ	Information/instructions for the facilitator/producer.
🗣	Say this...
👂	Anecdote to be told from your own experience to illustrate point.
🔑	Make these key points.
🕐	The time, in minutes, it typically takes to deliver this topic. This will vary depending on the interaction level of participants. Be aware of any time zone changes with participants when referencing a specific time.

You will see three columns. The first column represents the slide and timing, the second is for the facilitator, and the third for the producer. The headers will represent new slides/content as you move through the class.

NOTE to facilitator: Remember to ask for questions as appropriate. <u>Always</u> include technical directions, that is, please raise your hands, use the chat box, and so forth.

NOTE to producer: Annotations in producer column serve as a guideline. Producer should feel free to alternate highlighter colors, vary pointer icons, use boxes, squares, circles, and other visual tools desired.

IMPORTANT: Both the facilitator and producer involved in class should familiarize themselves with this material (slides and IG) prior to actual delivery.

SELECTION TRAINING		
DESCRIPTION, TIMING, MEDIA	**FACILITATOR NOTES**	**PRODUCER NOTES**
Pre-Event Warm-UP 🕐: **15 minutes before start of "class"** ┌─────────┐ │ Welcome │ └─────────┘ **Slide 1 welcome**	ⓘ Welcome participants! 🗣 **SAY**: îMany of us have been doing selection interviewing for years. This unit is designed to provide you with an update and perhaps offer a few new ideas. We encourage you to share your experiences with the group. You can tell us what works and what doesn't. We'll brush up on specific skills and review changes in employment law."	ⓘ Welcome participants and conduct audio checks. CHAT Activity 🗣 **SAY**: "While we wait to begin, please type in chat your own comments about the selection process. What have you found difficult or challenging in choosing new employees?"

SELECTION TRAINING		
DESCRIPTION, TIMING, MEDIA	**FACILITATOR NOTES**	**PRODUCER NOTES**
Agenda 🕐 **5 minutes** [Objectives] **Slide 2** **Objectives**	🗣 **SAY:** "Please turn to page one and read the objectives listed. As you read, please circle the numbers of the objectives that are of importance to you." ❓ **Ask:** "What questions are there about the objectives before we move on?" Give people a chance to raise their hand and discuss, then move on.	ⓘ Start session recording. Producer type in chat: "Page 1 of your workbook."
🕐 **10 minutes** [Survey 1.___ 2.___ 3.___] **Slide 3** **Survey Questions**	🗣 **SAY:** "Let's start by looking at your current current skill level. Please take a look at the survey on page 2 of your workbook. We'll do an online poll together, then you will use this information to set individualized goals on page 3."	Producer type in chat: "Page 2" Start poll

Tool 56. Instructor Guide Template: Teleconference

Contributed by Jennifer Hofmann and Nanette Miner, Ed.D.

To be engaging and to help break the monotony of one speaker's voice, an effective teleconference often takes a talk-show-type format; that is, a question-and-answer exchange between the trainer and a "host" and/or learners. The trainer and host should work together on a set of eight to ten seed questions to ensure a smooth session. Since there are no visuals in the teleconference environment, consider e-mailing handouts or note-taking outlines to learners prior to the teleconference.

Timing	Topic	Call Host/Activity	Production Notes
			Periodically welcome attendees and announce that you will be starting in X minutes. Be sure to start on time. Mute phone if too much background noise.
00 — :03	Start the call	Announce title/purpose of call Introduce yourself/credentials Introduce guest speaker(s) and have them respond Announce objectives/agenda for session Tell participants when you will stop for Q&A (generally at 20 minutes and 45 minutes into the call if a one-hour call). Alert participants to the fact that the phones are muted and how to un-mute them in order to ask a question.	

Timing	Topic	Call Host/Activity	Production Notes
:03 — :20	Begin Interview	Ask the first question. Ask follow-on questions as you deem necessary. Continue with half of the seed questions; then pause for Q&A from participants.	
:20 — :30	Q & A	Ask participants to be succinct in order to accommodate as many questions as possible. Ask questioner to identify him/herself. Always thank questioner for question/contribution.	
:30 — :45	Continue Interview	Continue with remaining seed questions.	
:45 — :55	Q & A	Ask participants to be succinct in order to accommodate as many questions as possible. Ask questioner to identify him/herself. Always thank questioner for question/contribution.	
:55 — :60	Conclude the call	Thank the guest speaker(s). Thanks the participants for their participation and insightful questions. Give participants instructions to ask follow-on questions if possible (e.g., Send an email to. . .). Say "Goodbye everyone."	Stay on the line until you are sure everyone has successfully exited the teleconference line.

Tool 57. Instructor Guide Template for a Video Conference Featuring a Guest Speaker

Contributed by Jennifer Hofmann and Nanette Miner, Ed.D.

A videoconference typically includes one site from which the program is broadcast with one or more additional sites in which learners gather to view the broadcast. Each site should have a conference host/moderator who knows the technology inside and out in order to keep things running smoothly and to make the guest speakers look their best.

Timing	Topic	Leader	Activity	Production Notes
15 minutes prior to start	Pre-Event			*Periodically welcome attendees and announce that you will be starting in XX minutes.* *Be sure to start on time.*
3 to 5 minutes	Welcome and introduce speaker	Verbally welcome everyone to the session and acknowledge each site in attendance Announce the topic and objective(s) of the session Remind attendees of any ground rules: How to mute phones; How to ask a question; How to set video conference (focus, telephoto position)		

Timing	Topic	Leader	Activity	Production Notes
		Announce tech support number and/or number to the main site Introduce the speaker		
15 to 20 minutes	Topic of the event		Speaker addresses group	*Support speaker as necessary; operate video conference TVs, PC, and micro-phone/polycoms.* *Write down questions/ answers and action items so speaker does not have to.*
5 to 10 minutes	Q & A	Ask each site for questions Rotate sites Include all sites		
15 to 20 minutes	Topic of the event		Speaker addresses group	*Support speaker as necessary; operate video conference TVs, PC, and micro-phone/poly-coms. Write down questions/ answers and action items so speaker does not have to.*

Timing	Topic	Leader	Activity	Production Notes
10 minutes	Wrap-Up	Thank speaker Provide contact information to audience if appropriate Tell attendees how they might access support materials used during the conference (slides, handouts, etc.) Tell sites how to sign off of video conference.		

Tools and Tips for Online Training

What's called "e-learning" can take a number of forms, from stand-alone asynchronous tutorials, to a "blended" format involving both asynchronous work and face-to-face classroom sessions, to synchronous meeting-format sessions. As this book is targeted more at classroom trainers than e-learning designers, contributors have offered some tools and tips to support the role the trainer will likely play in "e-learning": helping with design and supporting blended or multi-week facilitated online courses. Also, be sure to see Tool 48, a map of ideas matching online (and other) learning activities with learning styles and preferences.

Tips for What Learners Want: Developing Successful Online Learning Programs

Contributed by Mitchell Weisburg

1. **"I want meaningful instruction, not just books put online."** You cannot take a lecture or a book, put it online, and expect people to learn. People do not have the patience to turn pages, listen to a talking head, or watch a self-running demonstration. Internet learners want to see, hear, and do, often at the same time. They want to interact anywhere they can find an Internet connection. And they don't want to wait, even with a slow connection.

2. **"I want to learn what I want, when I want it, wherever I happen to be."** Convenience is critical. You can't expect someone to go through a whole course on a topic just because that's the way it's been taught in the past. Internet learners expect learning chunks of five to fifteen minutes. Think short attention spans, YouTube generation, and just-in-time learning.

3. **"How am I doing?"** Feedback is critical. It's not just about putting the information out there. Learners want to know how they are doing. And it's not just, "Did I get this answer right?," but, "How do I master this technique from now on?"

4. **"I learn it my way."** Sometimes a learner just needs a tip, sometimes a complete explanation. Often a learner will want to see an example. Many times a learner will want to practice. The choice has to be his or hers. A learner will not be held hostage just because a system only allows one style of learning; he or she will just tune out.

5. **"There's more than one way to get there."** Just as learners want to see material presented in different ways, so do they want choices about how to navigate the content. There isn't just one way to get to Carnegie Hall and there can't be just one path through the learning material. Some people will want to view an index. Some will want to search. Some will follow a series of links, and others will follow along sequentially. The key point is that the system and material have to be designed with multiple paths in mind.

6. **"Create once, use many times."** Learning offerings have to capitalize on materials that have been created for other purposes. Tutorials, lessons, and multimedia that are created for one application have to be able to be repackaged and made available for others. This is how to keep costs down.

7. **"Don't make me a hostage of Tech Support."** Keep it simple. Watch how people use your system and see where they fall down. Then build easier ways to interact and provide easy to access self-help. No one wants to email for support or call congested help lines. Make learning intuitive.

8. **"Things change."** Procedures become obsolete, new tasks require different skill sets, and errors must be corrected. Build easy ways to manage, correct, edit, change, and re-use your lessons, practice exercises, and questions.

9. **"Give me customized experiences."** It's not just important to track and measure how well people are learning. Use this information to personalize the learners' experience. Provide custom feedback, give advice, and recommend activities depending on the skills and goals of the learners and the course.

10. **"I want to stay connected."** Communicate and build a sense of community. Let learners know how they are doing and give them useful information on an ongoing basis. Find ways to bring them back.

Tips for Creating Self-Paced Online Courses

Contributed by Pete Blair

- Strive for stand-alone content, screen by screen.

- Design course navigation so that it is as intuitive as you can make it.

- Where possible, avoid automatically timed screen changes, unless those changes are timed to follow an audio script.

- Provide clues so that the learners will have some idea of what will happen when they do something.

- Select screen and text colors for a reason, and use those colors consistently throughout the course.

- Display the screen's relative location in the learning event.

- Provide "resume" function.

- Be cautious of humor.

- Provide easy access to a glossary throughout the learning event where applicable.

- Don't let screen design compete with learning!

Tool 58. Online Course Syllabus Template

Here is a syllabus template for communicating information to learners enrolled in multi-session courses. While it tends to look rather "academic," I find it very useful in supporting learners in my multi-week online courses. Many online course platforms (such as Moodle or BlackBoard—or Google and Yahoo! Groups, for those using Web communities to support courses) offer a place for instructors to store material—for instance, there are often separate links for items such as " course readings," "instructor contact information," and "technical requirements"—learners appreciate having all the information available in one place.

Start/End Dates:	
Instructor's Name:	
Office Location:	Building , room OR course website OR virtual office location (Elluminate, WebEx, etc.)
Office Hours:	00:00 – 00:00 Mon, Tues, Wed, Thurs, Fri
Office Phone:	000–0000
Email:	xxxx@xxxx.net
Online Chat:	Day, hour, access address
Instructor Web Page:	
Course Web Page:	
Class Hours:	00:00 – 00:00 Mon, Tues, Wed, Thurs, Fri (specify online, live, etc)
Prerequisite(s):	

A. Course Description

Provide one to two paragraphs describing the course. This should give learners an idea of the course content, overarching themes, and connections to work responsibilities. Realize that this item is what will help the learner decide whether the course is right for him or her. Why does the course exist? How will it contribute to the learner's professional growth?

B. Method of Instruction

This is a paragraph description indicating lecture, lecture/lab, group discussion, or other primary form of instruction; frequency or number of interim exams/quizzes; reading requirements; hands-on activities; field trips—basically, how the course described in Section A will be presented.

C. Course Objectives

Objective 1:

Objective 2:

Objective 3:

Objective 4:

Objective 5:

D. Course Topics/Units and Dates

1.

2.

3.

4.

5.

6.

E. Technology

Specify skills the learner will need, such as Web browsing and attaching documents to email.

Specify technology required:

Minimum operating system (i.e., Windows XP)

Printer

Email

Headset or microphone

Note any special software requirements such as installation of virtual classroom technology, etc.

All online courses will require Internet access; courses utilizing streaming video or Web meetings will require learner access to DSL or T1 Internet hookups.

If the course is online or blended, include an explanation of

- How the instructor will communicate with learners

- How the learners will communicate with each other

- How online participation will be assessed

- How the instructor will monitor online activities

- The level of technical competence required

- On-site meeting requirements, if any

F. Textbook(s) and Required Tools or Supplies

Be clear about where texts and readings can be acquired. Realize that online booksellers often only stock a few copies of any title; learners may find it better to order through the publisher.

- Textbook (required): *TITLE* and author

- Textbook (recommended): *TITLE* and author

- Supplies and/or tools: Specify item, size, quantity, and color.

G. Grading and Attendance Requirements

Clarify how you will determine whether the learner has satisfied completion requirements. This should include details on how competency-based requirements will be evaluated, how difficult-to-quantify things such as effort, improvement, and participation will be assessed, and what is expected in terms of attendance and participation.

H . Course Specifics

Explain any policies or procedures pertaining to assignments, discussions, expected participation, research form, or guidelines. Give dates and deadlines of assignments and dates of tests.

Describe what is happening in class. (It is often a good idea to indicate that the schedule is tentative and subject to change.) Learners will do better with tests and assignments when given a clear and stable sense of due dates so that they can plan their time accordingly. Make sure to **bold**, <u>underline</u>, or *highlight* significant due dates for assignments, tests. Consider providing a separate list of all the major assignments and their due dates, perhaps on an online calendar. Also include in your syllabus dates of special events, guest speakers, and holidays.

I. Other Policies and Safety

Include references to the organization's policies on sexual harassment, ADA/reasonable accommodation policies. If coursework is inherently dangerous, safety instructions and tests are required before any equipment may be used. Safety rules should be listed in the syllabus or in an attachment to it. Safety rules must also be posted, and safety tests taken by learners must be kept until the learners have completed or otherwise left the program.

J. Miscellaneous (As Needed or Desired)

- Suggestions for success

- Student personal data needed; privacy policies

- Course/instructor evaluations

- References and study sheets

- Permission forms; outlines of liability issues

Tool 59. Principles of Online Design Checklist

Contributed by Academic Media and Technology Services, Florida Gulf Coast University

Here's a tool meant especially for those delivering multi-week or academic-style courses. It would be particularly useful for those working with a course management platform like Blackboard, Moodle, Sakai, and those using a free online community, such as Google Groups or Yahoo Groups, for course management purposes.

Instructional Design Principles	Criteria
Learner Analysis	_____ Educational prerequisites are listed. _____ Entry-level knowledge/skills are described. _____ Technology skills are clearly articulated.
Course Goals/Objectives	_____ Course objectives are stated. _____ Objectives include measurable criteria. _____ Course expectations are described.
Instructional Activities	_____ Active learning strategies are employed to achieve objectives. _____ Activities are clearly linked to course objectives. _____ Information is chunked or segmented in a way that clarifies the content presented. _____ Materials are correctly cited.
Student and Course Evaluation	_____ Formative evaluation is provided through ongoing feedback. _____ Summative evaluation is clearly described.
Teaching Strategies	_____ The instructor guides learners to resources using a learner-centered philosophy. _____ Learners are engaged in active learning strategies. _____ A syllabus with course description, assignments, grading criteria, and resources is available.

Interaction and Feedback Principles	Criteria
Interaction Among Learners	Facilitates communication electronically through: required discussion, chat, or email and learner assignments.
Learner/Instructor Interaction	_____ Instructor email, office hours, and phone number are clearly identified on website. _____ Learners are encouraged to communicate electronically.
Learner/Materials Interaction	_____ Online technology orientation and/or self-readiness assessments are made available to Learners. _____ Links or content are provided for resources such as technology/software tutorials; online skills assessment; interaction protocol and expectations.
Electronic Collaboration	_____ Tools for collaboration are provided (bulletin board, email, telephone, etc). _____ Goals for online collaboration are stated. _____ Evaluation of collaboration is described.
Feedback Systems	_____ Modes of feedback are described. _____ Time duration for electronic feedback is provided. _____ Feedback timelines are described.
Paced Learning to Prevent Procrastination	_____ A schedule of assignments is provided.
Communication Asynchronous Synchronous	_____ Communication tools are clearly described. _____ A statement clarifies expectations about the frequency of student participation.
Incorporating Media Principles	Criteria
Information Presentation	_____ Information is logically grouped or chunked. _____ Scrolling is minimized or facilitated with anchors. (Learners would rather click to another screen than scroll on a single page.) _____ Shorter lines of text are used.

	_____ Information that orients users is readily apparent (i.e., banner, menu).
	_____ Screen size accommodates various platforms (i.e., webTV).
	_____ Information navigation is clear and consistent.
	_____ Site complies with university accessibility policy.
Interface Design	_____ Multiple techniques are used to highlight the current location.
	_____ Navigation cues are readily identifiable and consistently available.
	_____ Consistent layout design orients users throughout the site.
	_____ Hyperlinks are clearly identifiable.
	_____ Graphic elements and color serve an instructional purpose.
	_____ Graphic elements load quickly and read clearly.
	_____ Font type, size, and color are readable and consistent throughout the site.
	_____ Light text on dark background is used only as a design element, not to deliver lengthy text-based information.
Multimedia Elements	_____ Audio or video is clearly audible/visible.
	_____ Plug-in links are provided as needed.
	_____ Audio is not the sole carrier of instruction; audio enhances instruction.
	_____ Animation is used to draw attention; non-stop animation elements are avoided.
	_____ Video is accessible to learners; video enhances instruction; video clips are short (5 to 25 seconds).
	_____ Multimedia elements do not exceed organization's minimum hardware/software requirements.

Chapter 3 Wrap-Up

Once design of a new program is nearing completion it's important to go back and review; problems caught now are easier to correct than they will be once train-the-trainer efforts are underway. Tool 59 offers suggestions for reviewing design for online programs. Here are two more tools, one quick, one more detailed, for reviewing your design for classroom training.

Tool 60. Training Design Checklist: Quick Version

Contributed by Results Through Training (www.RTTWorks.com)

Finished and in a hurry? Look back over your final instructional plan and see whether you can answer "yes" to all of the following:

- Do you have a variety of activities/methods throughout the design?

- Is lecture limited to no more than 10 minutes at a time?

- Do you have a method for measuring how well objectives are met in each section?

- Have you identified the support materials needed for each activity?

- Do your content and activities reflect the objectives for a given section?

- Are all objectives addressed in some activity?

- Are time estimates realistic for the size group you anticipate?

- Does your plan include an activity around application to the job?

- Are content descriptions detailed enough to communicate the overall goal and structure of an activity?

Tool 61. Training Design Checklist: Comprehensive Version

Contributed by Results Through Training (www.RTTWorks.com)

Here's a more extensive version of the checklist in Tool 60, particularly useful for those newer to training and training design.

Opening

- Have you included a statement of objectives in the opening?

- Do you have an icebreaker that relates to the training topic?

- Is the length of the icebreaker appropriate for the length of the training (longer training can support a longer icebreaker)?

Objectives

- Have you identified specific and measurable objectives for each section of the training program?

- Is each objective addressed in the content for that section?

Content

- Is there a clear link between each piece of content and at least one training objective?

- Is the time realistic for complex content areas?

- Is the content appropriate and at the right level of detail for the target audience?

- Is there a transition from one piece of content to another explaining how the two are related?

Methods

- Have you avoided more than 10 minutes of lecture at a time?

- Have you avoided repetitive training methods (e.g., lecture, paired exercise, lecture, paired exercise, lecture, paired exercise)?

- Do your methods include individual, paired, small group, and large group activities?

- Is there a lively activity within the first hour after lunch?

- Do you have methods that reach a variety of learning styles?

Timing

- Have you estimated time for each piece of content, rather than for a complete section?

- Are times realistic for each piece of content?

- When estimating time for an activity, did you include the time it takes to explain and debrief the activity?

- Did you include time to answer questions in each section?

- Are time estimates realistic based on the size of the group you anticipate?

Resources/Support Materials

- Do you have reference materials for any complex or new content areas?

- Do you have visual support for any key messages or content?

- Are you using flip charts or posters for content you want to reference repeatedly in the training?

- Are you using slides for content you will address for just a short time?

- Are you using written instructions for any activities?

Closing

- Have you included a summary of learning in the closing? Does the closing include an action plan or some type of activity to drive application of training?

Additional Suggested Resources

For further exploration of particular techniques, see Jean Barbazette's *Instant Case Studies* (Pfeiffer, 2004) and Mary Wacker and Lori Silverman's *Stories Trainers Tell* (Pfeiffer, 2002). Allison Rossett is the field's leading expert on job aids; her 1991 *Handbook of Job Aids* (Pfeiffer, 1991) is a classic. And Patti Shank's *The Online Learning Idea Book* (Pfeiffer, 2007) offers good ideas for evaluating the quality of learner interactions and discussions in the online environment.

CHAPTER 4

Implement

N ow is the time to deliver the instruction. Trainers who will provide the training need to be prepared and given time to rehearse; training is officially "piloted," although much could be done before this point to test and validate materials and approaches. Training management issues, such as logistics, like scheduling rooms, ordering materials, and marketing programs, happen here as well.

This phase also includes the in-the-trenches delivery and facilitation of the instruction. Included here are tips for managing training interactions, from the characteristics of excellent facilitators to dealing with the challenging and outright hostile.

The first two sections cover critical skills for trainers and dealing with challenging situations. A number of the tips for effective facilitation here will look familiar to seasoned trainers. There are dozens of good books on facilitation skills (many on the subject of "dealing with difficult behaviors" alone); novice trainers are encouraged to read up and practice as much as possible. But strong facilitation takes practice, and experience, and time—and a willingness, sometimes, to take calculated risks. The last section in this chapter offers organizer tools and tips for dealing with the stresses unique to trainers, and ends with tips for the person working as the organization's "Lone Ranger" trainer.

Critical Trainer Skills

Success in the classroom does not come only from strict adherence to a detailed instructor guide. Other factors, such as attention to preparation, skill in facilitating groups, and care taken to approach learners with the right tone, will have an impact on the learners and the session. The contributors for this section have done their best to distill their own experiences and lessons learned into quick guidelines for those newer to the field (and that could serve as reminders for those of us who aren't so new).

5 Areas of Preparation

Contributed by Jan Haverkamp

Preparation involves much more than ordering handouts and setting up tables and chairs. Here are some suggestions for additional areas of preparation vital to a successful experience.

1. Prepare the *Process*

It is vital to prepare the process most likely to achieve the results the client desires and to anticipate the need to be flexible. Writing out a script for what you plan to say will give you the opportunity to "test drive" material and think through choosing the best possible approach. This is important, even for those working from a scripted lesson plan: *how* you say something is often as important as *what* you say. It will also help align your subconscious with the way you behave in front of the group, minimizing the chance of sending mixed messages.

2. Prepare for the *Group*

It is important to get a feel for the group and its social dynamics. Often you may only be able to talk with the group leader in advance of the session. Try, if you can, to talk to all of the participants, or at least a representative mix of them. This will help you develop a tacit understanding of the group and the personalities and issues involved.

3. Prepare *Yourself*

This is critical, and may even be more important than the first two. You must be aware of your deepest intention toward the client. Do you really want them to succeed? Naturally, the obvious unreflective answer is, "Yes." But watch out for your own hidden agendas, prejudices, and stresses. Are you delighted with the assignment? Are you detached from the outcomes of the workshop? Do you "believe" in the content? You get the idea.

4. Prepare the *Space*

Consider the room and facilities. Don't think of this as only setting up equipment and chart stands, but about creating a physical environment that encourages learning.

5. Prepare the *Materials*

The last bit of preparation is that of materials and handouts. Materials should be designed to enable learners to be effective during the class, to be useful after the class, and to function as symbols of the session.

Tips for Giving Instructions

Contributed by Jane Bozarth, Patti Shank, and Cindy Epps

- Ask participants to repeat what they are supposed to do.

- Give/show an exemplar of what you want (worked examples).

- Have people peer review each others' work before sharing with rest of class.

- Ask why this is being done (activate metacognition).

- Make sure *you* know what you want them to do: asking twenty people to break into four groups of five is different from asking them to break into five groups of four. Be clear.

- If people will be working on an activity in groups, move them first into their groups and then give the instructions.

- Practice, practice, practice.

- Give an overview of what you'll be doing, what you expect, and then give step-by-step instructions.

- Pay attention to the learners. Let them give you cues if they are confused, with you, etc.

- Give them an example (personal, past experience, etc.).

- If appropriate, show them a possible end product so they'll have a visual conception.

- Give clear timeframes.

Incredible Credibility

Contributed by Terrence Gargiulo

There's that moment at the beginning of every class when we think to ourselves, "Quick! Say something to prove to these folks that you belong up here." Everyone has to establish credibility with a group. Our credibility is about our believability. We already have the authority; standing in front of a group naturally grants us a certain position. Now our challenge lies in winning the trust and respect of others. We need to be accessible to our learners, sensitive to their needs, and responsive to satisfying their learning objectives.

Be a Good Host

Your credibility begins the moment you interact with learners. First impressions are the most important ones. Do everything you can to make people feel comfortable. Little things make a big difference. I can remember times, for instance, when I have gone out of my way to find a more comfortable chair for an injured person.

Be Personable

Smiles are a wonderful way to break the ice. They will relax you and encourage people to interact with you before an event begins. There is nothing worse than walking into a training venue and mistaking it for a library. Encourage conversation by taking an interest in people. When appropriate, share a little tidbit about yourself without dominating the conversation.

It's All in the Doing

Learners grant credibility based on your performance. To quote a favorite cliché, "actions speak louder than words." Treat every interaction and question asked as an opportunity to demonstrate competence. Let your expertise shine through your command of the material.

Tell a Story

People love stories. Use a story to share an experience. It provides people with a concrete example of the material being learned and gives you an outlet to build credibility.

Discover Learners' Learning Objectives

It's all about them. Uncover a learner's needs, demonstrate your capability to fulfill those needs, and you will win his or her respect every time. Our credibility as trainers is linked directly to the learning objectives of learning. When we help them achieve their learning objectives, we both stand to win.

Manage Your Learning Commitments

Disappointment hurts. Temper your enthusiasm to transfer as much learning as you can with an honest evaluation of what is possible given the constraints of the training. Be sure to under-promise and over-deliver. Treat learning commitments as liabilities. Pay them off diligently and your assets of credibility will never be in danger.

Give Credit to Others

You look good when you make others look good. Nobody likes a know-it-all, and nobody can know everything. Be willing to share the podium figuratively and if necessary literally. Your credibility will be enhanced by the company you keep.

The Seven Principles of Facilitation

Contributed by Nina Coil

A participant in a multi-week facilitation skills course I teach posted the following message on the course blog: "I am afraid of open discussion and would like to feel more comfortable with that." Nina Coil of Linkage, Inc., offers the following advice:

1. Be Courageous

Good facilitation is about taking risks. By inviting challenges that enrich the learning experience, and handling the unpredictable dynamics of human interaction, you build your own comfort, confidence, and competence.

An experienced facilitator knows to let go of the need to be in complete control. Allowing yourself to go out of your own comfort zone and embracing an appropriate level of risk is critical to real learning for the group, and for yourself as facilitator. Try new activities and explore new topics.

- Invite challenge and disagreement from your audience, in both the content and facilitation.

- Embrace the complexity of your subject and know your own limits; acknowledge that you do not have all of the answers.

- Acknowledge and welcome the challenge of an audience with diverse opinions, backgrounds, and attitudes.

- Challenge your audience in order to enhance their learning. Push them beyond their comfort zone through your facilitation of the content.

Think back to the last time you felt anxious while facilitating a group process. What felt risky to you in this situation? What benefits could the group have derived from your willingness to "hang in there"?

Above all, how can you remind yourself in the moment that the learning experience you are facilitating is about *them*, not *you*, in order to refocus your energy outward to their learning needs?

2. Be a Role Model

As a facilitator of training, you have a dual responsibility to model both learning *and* leading. As a learner, you must model active participation and openness to your own growth. If you are eager to enhance your own learning experience, through a respect for the participants' knowledge and contributions, the audience will respond in kind. Your own energy, curiosity, interest in and enjoyment of the subject and in your participants should provide a strong example to the group.

You are also a leader in the sense of "walking the talk." If you are facilitating a module on masterful communication skills, make sure that you use open-ended questions and genuinely listen to the responses which emerge. If you are facilitating a module on coaching, use your coaching framework as you work with the participants during the session. Being a role model of the leader-learner will earn you respect and credibility from your participants, while demonstrating the value of the subject matter being explored.

Consider the last time you felt bored leading a session. Think about why that might have been the case—were you taking up too much air time yourself, without involving the participants? If you felt defensive at any point, consider how you might have shared your reaction with participants in furtherance of their own learning. Discomfort is a natural part of the learning process, and this holds true for the facilitator as well as for the audience.

3. Balance Flexibility and Responsibility

A critical component of exceptional facilitation is the ability to read and interpret (accurately) the needs of the participants, and to make adjustments accordingly. Being spontaneous and flexible to concerns and issues that emerge will benefit both you and the group. Rigidly adhering to your timetable despite clear indications that there is an issue to be dealt with will prevent the participants from concentrating on the learning activities you had planned. You must meet the group where they are, even if that means adjusting your thoughtful plan for the day.

At the same time, you must deliver on your promise to meet the stated learning objectives and overall timeframes of the program. It is critical that you remain mindful of the passage of time, and that you manage your own reactions to challenging participant behaviors. Nothing can drain the life out of a group more surely than an overemphasis on the needs of one participant. The group relies on you to see to it that their time is well spent. If you digress from the timeframes you had planned, it must be for a significant learning purpose, and with the explicit approval of the group.

Think about the last time you facilitated a group learning experience during which you felt conflicted as to whether to digress or to adhere to the agenda. What did you end up doing, and why? How could you have involved the group in your decision? How might that have modeled one of the behaviors in your leadership program?

4. Make It Theirs

Value what learners bring to the workshop. Adult learners need and deserve to be respected for their life experience and knowledge. As a facilitator, encouraging participation and asking appropriately probing questions can open a wealth of resources for everyone in the room.

Build in ways to maximize participants' input, through discussion of workplace issues, paired and small group coaching and feedback, sharing of best practices, advice-swapping sessions, and networking opportunities.

Making full use of participants' experience is a key component to a successful learning process. The best facilitators are adept at drawing this out, then storing it and resurfacing it at later points in the training. Synthesizing the comments shared in the room, within the learning framework you have created, will enable the participants to feel valued while increasing the genuine transfer of their learning back to the workplace.

Think back to a learning experience in which the participants felt they were being asked to learn a "foreign language." Consider whether there might have been ways to build in more participant involvement in the naming of constructs, the descriptions of elements, and the sharing of experiences that illustrate concepts and principles in action. After all, if the participants have not made the learning their own, in their own words, it will not leave the room, and everyone's time and effort has been wasted.

5. Make It Yours

In order to be a dynamic facilitator, you must be authentic. Your effectiveness is heightened when you connect with the material and personalize it so that you are fully comfortable and truly engaged in front of your group.

When you are passionate about the material, you foster learning and passion in others. The energy that you put into making the material yours, by accessing your own work and life experience as you prepare to facilitate, will emanate to your audience and improve your facilitation skills immensely. Be wary of including too many of your own "war stories"—participants can be encouraged to share their own when needed. But if you cannot "riff" on the material you are sharing with the group, you have not done your homework, and the learning outcomes will suffer.

When was the last time you facilitated a learning experience and felt either out of your depth or left cold by the content? What might you have done to increase your connection to the material? What value would the participants have gained from your own genuine enthusiasm for or deep understanding of the concepts and practices you were sharing with them?

6. Focus on Application

Learners need to apply what they have learned in order to understand how to use it in their daily work. As a facilitator you must ensure that the participants fully grasp the content and can articulate its relevance, in their own words, so that they can translate the learning into new skills and improved performance.

Well-designed workshops incorporate a substantial amount of skill-building practice and application. This is particularly critical in the development of soft skills, which, to be effective, must be practiced live, to desensitize and prepare the learner to try out the new behaviors in real life.

Practice sessions should never be shortchanged. If you must make adjustments due to time constraints, cut your own "air time" first. Carve out as much time as possible in the agenda for participants to work with and confirm the applicability of all new content and learning.

Not all participants will be equally engaged with all of the methodologies you build into your programming. Some will need discussion time, others will require an opportunity to read, reflect, and plan, still others will be reluctant to engage in role plays or simulations. But unless you incorporate elements of all of these approaches into your learning experience, the learning will evanesce. "Use it or lose it" pertains as much to learning experiences as to the development of Olympic-level athletic ability.

Think back to the last time you led a learning session. Did the participants have an opportunity to try out the behaviors you were advocating? Did they have time to reflect on their insights and to make a realistic plan to act on their insights? How might you have built in more application activities?

7. Link It to the Business

Training events do not occur in a vacuum. You must have a solid understanding of how the training that you are providing connects with the business goals, performance objectives, issues, and challenges of your audience. Using this context as a foundation, and assisting participants to make this connection, establishes credibility and fosters buy-in.

We strongly recommend that you contact each participant prior to the workshop to better understand his or her specific issues and motivation for taking the course, as well as his or her role and level of experience.

For internal trainers, the more you know about how your organization's strategy, operations, and culture, the more effective and credible you will be. Additionally, you should know how any single course aligns with the overall framework of the organization's management or leadership training initiatives.

After all, if you can't convincingly articulate the bottom-line value of the work you are doing, and of the time these high level executives are spending with you, who will do it for you?

No one said this work would be easy. In fact, there are days when each of us, if we are honest, wonder why on earth we have chosen to take on the challenge of facilitating learning experiences in which we must model what we would ask of our own leaders. But if we truly believe in the value and the possibility of developing inspiring leaders with wisdom, compassion, and clarity of purpose, we must hold this belief of ourselves, as well.

Tool 62. Mapping Discussion Flow

Contributed by Nancy K. Gustafson, Ed.D.

The interaction map explained here is a remarkably powerful tool for evaluating interaction among and between trainer and learners, facilitator and participants, and in other meeting situations such as managers and staff. I have used it with dramatic results in helping new trainers work toward improvement in their presentation and facilitation skills. (I also recommend it as an occasional exercise for experienced trainers as well. Having someone map you as you lead a session may provide eye-opening information about your own strengths and tendencies.) Important: It is difficult and distracting, for both trainer and learners, for the trainer to try to lead a discussion while drawing the map. Using this technique effectively requires a "third-party mapper." That is, have a colleague map the session you are leading, or you serve as the mapper for the manager wanting feedback on her effectiveness at leading meetings, and so forth.

A picture is worth a thousand words. The best way to get feedback on our actions and behaviors as facilitators is to see for ourselves what we look like in action. We can video ourselves, yet that is often cumbersome and intimidating. Another way to visualize our actions as facilitators is to draw a discussion map. This puts on paper the trail between facilitator and participants, and between participants. Discussion is a powerful teaching strategy when the balance of conversation is appropriate for the stage of learning. Viewing this picture allows the facilitator to analyze and determine:

- Is the balance of communication between me, the facilitator, and participants appropriate at this stage in the learning?

- Is the facilitator the hub of the conversation with questions/comments coming from and being directed to the facilitator? Is this appropriate at this stage in the learning? Or should participants be discussing the learning with each other more of the time?

- Are all participants contributing at an appropriate level? Who is dominating the conversation? Who has not contributed much or at all?

- Is any participant routinely interrupting another? Is any participant routinely being interrupted?

To create a discussion map, take a piece of paper or flip-chart paper and record the room arrangement. Identify who is sitting where, including participants, facilitator, guests—anyone who might speak. Then, as conversation begins, draw arrows to reflect who is saying what to whom, and how:

- Draw an arrow from the facilitator to the middle of the room if a general question/statement to the group at large is asked/said. Add tick marks to that arrow for subsequent questions/comments.

- Draw an arrow from the facilitator to a specific participant if a question or comment is directed to that individual rather than the group. Add tick marks for subsequent comments.

- Draw an arrow from a participant to the middle of the room if a general question/statement to the group at large is asked/said. Add tick marks for subsequent comments.

- Draw an arrow from a participant to the facilitator if a question or comment is directed to the facilitator rather than the group. Add tick marks for subsequent comments.

- Draw an arrow from one participant to another if a question or comment is directed from one participant to another participant.

- Indicate a statement that was interrupted by placing a dash across the arrow, making something like a "t." This will let you know who is being interrupted.

- Place a star, or some other mark, next to the individual who interrupted.

Mapping a discussion for only 10 or 15 minutes can help a facilitator "see" what the communication flow looks like and determine its appropriateness. Looking at Discussion Map A, it appears that:

- Discussion was predominantly facilitator-led.

- Participant 8 talked most of the time.

- Several participants made no comments (2, 4, 6, 7, 12, 13, 14).

- The facilitator cut off Participant 3 once.

- Participants 10 and 11 had a conversation between themselves.

The point of this analysis is to determine risks or limitations to learning. Is it appropriate that the facilitator led the discussion? If it is early in the learning event, the facilitator may be giving a brief lecture. If it is near the end of the learning event, it may be more appropriate for the learners to be taking over the discussion. In that case, the conversation would look more like Discussion Map B.

- Participants are talking more to each other than to the facilitator.

- Most likely, the facilitator was asking follow-up questions to an individual or group to keep the dialog going.

- Everyone is engaged in the conversation.

- No one appeared to dominate the conversation.

By drawing a discussion map, a facilitator can get a lot of good information about the communication pattern occurring at any given time. The facilitator can then analyze the map to determine whether the discussion flow supports learning or if there are any risks to learning.

Discussion Map A

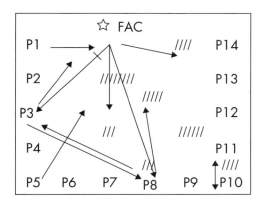

Discussion Map B

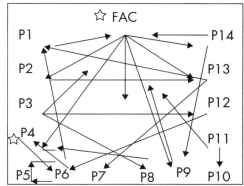

Tips for Using Props in Training

Submitted by Patti Shank, Jane Bozarth, Cindy Epps

- Ask yourself: Will this offend anyone? Rubber chicken: Probably ok. Enormous pair of women's underwear: Not ok.

- PRACTICE! Don't do magic tricks until and unless you can make them work right, every time.

- Ask learners to bring props.

- Use props only if they will enhance your point. Otherwise they will detract from your message.

- Make sure props are easily identifiable with your intent. If you are struggling to help your learners understand how the prop is related to your point, then you aren't using the right prop.

- Make it easy on yourself: Simple is better than complex, especially if you are traveling.

- The element of surprise can be essential: keep them out of sight until you need them.

- Quit talking and let the prop teach your point.

Tips for Marketing Your Training Programs

Contributed by Jennifer Hofmann, Patti Shank, Cindy Epps, Susan E. Nunn, Teri Armstrong, and Jane Bozarth

- Ask your subject-matter experts to help you spread the word about the learning initiative.

- Use appealing titles. "Verbal Judo" is more enticing than "Communication Skills."

- Make sure those appealing titles live up to their promises.

- Keep in touch with people who are excited about training. Have them share their experiences and talk about it with other departments, supervisors, and employees. Remember: Word of mouth is one of the most powerful ways to spread the news.

- Offer learners the opportunity to participate in and provide feedback about pilots of new programs.

- Create a theme or "campaign" for your learning initiative. The creative use of posters, table tents, fonts, colors, and logos can keep your campaign exciting. Keep the campaign organized and on a regular schedule.

- Send a regular weekly or monthly email so employees start to look forward to receiving it. Make sure the subject line of the email is attention grabbing so it does not get lost in the shuffle of emails that everyone receives.

- Occasionally offer something for free for which you would normally need to charge.

- Include a survey about potential training programs as part of your marketing campaign so you can identify issues that may be hot-buttons, unclear, or very popular. Feedback will help you learn what is and is not working.

- Have the company newsletter dedicate a specific section to training. Post regular updates, events, and milestones so that they can be shared with all employees.

- Create a "brand" for your training department. Create a logo and put it on everything you distribute, including workbooks, "Do Not Disturb" signs for online learners, certificates of completion, maybe even trainer T-shirts.

- Make the "What's in It for Me?" (WIIFM) message loud and clear. Provide information about why and how the training will benefit the participants.

- Create a meeting date so interested participants can come and ask questions about programs.

- Offer one free registration for a certain number of free referrals to your program.

- Ask participants for testimonials immediately after training. Make it part of the evaluation form. It is important to capture positive comments about the learning experience when emotions and satisfaction are high.

- Offer short "teaser" versions of longer programs.

Tips for Working with Multicultural Audiences

- Be careful of uniquely culture- or nation-specific references, such as "Excedrin Headache" and "Mind the Gap."

- Avoid sports analogies. Phrases like "three strikes" and "stepping up to the plate" mean nothing to people from other countries.

- Use gender-neutral language and names.

- Be sensitive to cultural issues regarding hierarchy and social position. Not all countries, for instance, value "equality" or the power of the individual.

- When in doubt, go with the more formal, rather than less formal, approach.

- If possible, have local SMEs or other experts review your design and presentation.

- If doing synchronous work, be mindful of time zones. Your 1 p.m. online class means someone in Paris will be driving home in rush hour traffic.

- Watch out for slang and idioms, such as "more than one way to skin a cat."

- Be careful of culture- and language-specific activities like crossword puzzles and word searches.

Tool 63. Trainer Skills Assessment

Designed for the workplace trainer wearing multiple hats of designer, facilitator, and technology expert, the North Carolina, USA, Certified Training Specialist Course requires a score of "2" or better on all areas of this score sheet (adapted from an original document from the NC Justice Academy) to attain the designation of "Certified Training Specialist."

Trainer Skills Assessment

Candidate: _____ Assessor: _____ Date: _____

Topic: _____ Time Started: _____ Time Finished: _____

Presentation Evaluation Criteria

Rating System: 0 = Did Not Do/Unacceptable   1 = Marginal   2 = Acceptable   3 = Above Average

Performance Factors	Guidelines for Performance Ratings
Voice Quality	**Voice Quality**
Easy to listen to and understand	0 = Inarticulate, inaudible, reads to learners
Comments:	1 = Monotonous, breathy, high-pitched; stilted
	2 = Adequate volume; voice may fade some
	3 = Well-modulated, appropriate variety; conveys enthusiasm
Verbal Skills	**Verbal Skills**
Uses standard mainstream English and grammar. Limits jargon to the learners' field.	0 = Non-standard grammar and vocabulary; frequent mispronunciations
	1 = Slippage in grammar and usage; repeats cliches; slang, jargon; oks, uhs
Comments:	2 = Articulate; few usage errors; appropriate inflection/emphasis; may be formal
	3 = Speaks precisely; conversational tone; good word choice
Appearance	**Appearance**
Grooming	0 = Poor dress/grooming; no eye contact; distracting mannerisms; awkward movements
Gestures	1 = Passable dress and grooming; stays in one spot; some eye contact; distracting mannerisms, movement may be stiff or excessive
Eye Contact	2 = Neat/well-groomed; gestures natural; maintains eye contact; occasional distracting mannerisms, may show nervous energy
Movement	3 = Movement and gestures natural and purposeful; conversational eye contact, no distracting mannerisms; impeccable dress and grooming
Comments:	

Performance Factors	Guidelines for Performance Ratings
Personal Qualities of the Instructor	**Personal Qualities of the Instructor**
Selfless: ⇒ puts learner first ⇒ subordinates personal needs ⇒ sensitive to individual differences Poised Ethical Comments:	0 = Obviously nervous; self-focused; confused, no attempt to address learner styles and differences 1 = Self-conscious; thrown by minor problems; apparently nervous; polite but aloof or too friendly; apologizes too much; too formal. Plays the expert. 2 = Mostly focused on learners' needs and individual differences, but may slip into self-focus; may be thrown by minor problems; takes self too seriously; may take challenges personally; reserved. Understands and seeks to accommodate learner differences. 3 = Makes learner feel attended to and understood; unflappable, poised, tactful; great sense of humor. Learner more important than the lesson.
Training Aids	**Training Aids**
Use of writing surfaces and aids Relevance of aids Comments:	0 = Training aids inadequate; handled poorly; too many slides 1 = Grammar/spelling errors; sloppy writing on chart, awkward 2 = Aids illustrate points and support instruction; apparent preparation; aids well used 3 = Imaginative aids; smoothly displayed; integrated into lesson; enhance understanding
Q & A	**Q & A**
Uses questions strategically Encourages and facilitates learners in answering each others' questions Responds sufficiently to learners' questions Comments:	0 = Rhetorical questions only; learner questions discouraged/postponed till end; handles responses poorly; misunderstands learners' questions 1 = Delays learners' questions to fit lesson plan; sometimes misunderstands questions. Learners not given a chance to answer each others' questions 2 = Questions reasonably well formulated and clear to learners; learner questions handled adequately; uses learners for answers occasionally 3 = Socratic style for questions; facilitates learners answering each others' questions; avoids answering questions until learners' have tried

Learner Involvement

Learner Involvement	Learner Involvement
Plans for Participation	0 = Unable to get participation or unwilling to encourage participation; learners restless, inattentive, hesitant, or afraid to participate.
Maintains learners' attention	1 = Fails to elicit general interest and participation; depends on a few students for reaction; lapses in attention.
Comments:	2 = Interest aroused in most learners; balanced learner/trainer participation. Learners mostly attentive.
	3 = Participation free and steady; lapses in attention rare.

Organization

Organization	Organization
Starts and stops on time	0 = Seating arrangements inappropriate for size of group. Started late.
Appropriate seating.	1 = Some time fillers, inferior choice of seating arrangements.
Comments:	2 = Room and seating arrangement adequate. Manages time correctly.
	3 = Room and seating arrangements appropriate. Time well managed.

Planning

Planning	Planning
Plans for individual and group needs	0 = No apparent provision for individual differences; objectives undefined, unattainable; goes off track
Stays on track and on time	1 = Organization minimal; follows time guidelines loosely
Presents simple to complex	2 = Consideration of individual differences; simple to complex order emphasized; techniques appropriate; stays on time
Comments:	3 = Well organized; considers differences; good variety of materials/methods

Performance Factors	Guidelines for Performance Ratings
Lesson Introduction	**Lesson Introduction**
Opening statement Uses an appropriate attention getter Statement of objectives/purpose Reasons for learning	0 = Fails to secure attention; objectives not clearly stated; importance of material not mentioned; fails to relate instruction to preceding or succeeding lessons 1 = Secures class attention with considerable effort; superficially defines purpose and objectives; barely outlines scope of lesson 2 = Gets and holds attention; adequately defines objectives; outlines scope of lesson; stresses WIIFM 3 = Gets and holds attention effectively and effortlessly; explains objectives; stresses WIIFM; defines scope of lesson; relates lesson to related materials
Lesson Body	**Lesson Body**
Covers topic Presents information logically Transitions: smoothly with continuous progression and development of lesson. Encourages assessment of how learning can be applied to jobs; elicits examples of practice dilemmas and successes	0 = Dull/plodding; lectures and reads; fails to cover objectives or follow plan 1 = Abrupt transitions, reads notes often. Doesn't explain objectives; partially follows plan. 2 = Techniques appropriate but limited variety; attends to most students; uses notes well; usually smooth transitions; uses appropriate illustrations and examples; covers objectives adequately and follows lesson plan. 3 = Well organized, informative, good transitions, uses examples/illustrations effectively. Explains objectives; follows lesson plan. Summarizes throughout. Gives examples and facilitates assessment for applying information to jobs.
Conclusion	**Conclusion**
Summary of objective and learning points Transfer of learning Closing statement	0 = Weak or no summary 1 = Hurried, dry summary; superficially covers objectives 2 = Recaps teaching points and objectives. Closing calls to action. 3 = Powerful summary; reemphasizes learning points and ideas for transfer

Technology, Computer, and Distance Learning Skills

Operates, assembles, and makes emergency repairs to a/v equipment: LCD projector, computer, overhead projector, and TV/VCR	0 = Cannot correct equipment failure; no backup/alternative; no plan for design as online learning program. 1 = Apologizes for equipment failure, solves problem with significant disruption of class time. Provides token plan for offering content online.
Provides contingency plan with alternative methods if equipment fails	2 = Can make repairs; plan for offering online shows understanding of limits and capabilities of the online environment and assorted technologies.
Plans for redesigning lesson as standalone online program or blended learning event	3 = Seamlessly recovers from equipment failure. Plan for content online includes imaginative and/or collaborative strategies.

Transfer of Learning

Plans to offer activities to promote transfer before, during, and after training. Makes training process rather than event	0 = Fails to relate training to on the job application 1 = Makes perfunctory connections between training and work setting 2 = Repeatedly relates importance of new skill/information to trainee's role; shows understanding of trainees' work issues/setting/situations. Uses basic assessment strategies.
Acknowledges importance of management in training and takes steps to involve supervisors in pre- and post-training activities	3 = Plan includes strategies to involve management before/after training; designs post-training activities to support transfer; assesses trainees' understanding and performance; recommends development activities; shows understanding of trainees' work issues, setting, and situations and connects training and application on the job; offers assessments to evaluate training.
Understands barriers to new performance; provides ideas and strategies for overcoming them	

Dealing with Challenges

As trainers, it seems we all, sooner or later, find ourselves in an unexpected situation. Sometimes this comes in the form of a learner with especially challenging behaviors. Other times it is a situation involving a whole group. My most memorable unexpected challenge came when I went to deliver what had been requested as a very straightforward repeat of a lunchtime-learning "stress management" workshop I'd done for an organization. I arrived to find that the entire learner group was, due to budget cuts, being laid off with little promise of ever returning to their jobs. While the organization should have told me this when they made the request, and the learners should not have been sent to a basic overview of "stress management," the fact was that I was in the room, the learners were there, and they needed help. Expressing my anger with the organization and canceling the session would not do anything to support those learners. I fortunately do have a strong background in group facilitation, and in a prior job had taught "career planning and resume writing," so the learners and I were able to work together to reconfigure my lesson plan into a session more useful for them: managing the stress of job loss by creating realistic job-search strategies. This section includes suggestions for managing such situations, offered by seasoned trainers and facilitators who have tried to capture the essence of their "lessons learned."

Tips: Delivering an Unpopular Message

Contributed by R. Anne Hull and Dan Young

There are times when the trainer is delivering an unpopular message or teaching a procedure associated with an unpopular change. Learners will sometimes want to "shoot the messenger." Here are some tips for managing this situation.

Be Proactive

Prior to the session, clarify exactly what kind of feedback the company is prepared to accept and respond to. Trainers like to help people, and in situations in which the policy being trained is unpopular, trainers want to be sympathetic. They may make promises to take feedback back to management. Learners may raise legitimate points or concerns that the trainer has not anticipated, and the natural reaction of the trainer is, "Good point. I'll take that back to management and see what I can learn about it. No promises, but I will make sure your voice is heard."

In other words, trainers sometimes present a more flexible or negotiable view of the policy than management may allow. This can have an adverse impact for management (concerned that their message did not get across fully) and for the learners (who are waiting for their champion, the trainer, to bring their important point back to management). Clear expectations with regard to feedback channels is the key.

In the Session

1. Be sure that you, as the trainer, are doing everything "right" that is within your control: start and end the session on time, give breaks as appropriate, be confident about the topic, and be competent to demonstrate the skills being taught.

2. Begin with and maintain a positive, respectful attitude toward the topic and the learners.

3. Acknowledge that this may not be a popular program. Your role is to deliver the message, not to change or make decisions.

4. Determine how to best work together in this session [deal with potential disruptive behavior]:

- Develop and post a working agreement with each group to include not only the standard items such as cell phones silenced and timely return from breaks, but also how to voice an opinion appropriately and the importance of listening to others.

- Maintain professional courtesy when faced with hostility. Manage your own tendency toward defensiveness; acknowledge learners' feelings, don't discount them; ask for clarification and specificity to further understand their resistance.

- Post a sheet for questions that they would like to have answered.

- Do not guess. Determine whose role it is to find the answers [encourage participants to do as much for themselves as possible, don't take on their issues] and how to get responses to the participants.

5. When meeting resistance, gently probe to discern anything that needs to be brought to the decision-makers' attention. These sessions often reveal true bugs in the system.

6. Generally let the group decide how it wants to manage itself. Avoid the role of parent or disciplinarian. Encourage learners to monitor themselves.

When Difficult Issues Threaten Training

Contributed by Terrence Gargiulo

It is a given that effective training depends heavily on strong trainer facilitation skills. If you are a novice, work to develop your ability in managing groups and guiding discussions. Here are some guiding principles that contributor Terrence Gargiulo has found useful over the years.

Imagine the following scenario: You have been contracted by upper management to teach a communications and team-building workshop to a group of disgruntled union employees whom you have never worked with before. Morale is low. The union is in dispute with management. People are being laid off left and right, and there is a good chance that the plant will be closed.

How about this one? You find out minutes before you are to begin a workshop that a recently retired employee has just died. He or she was a long-time employee at this company and well known by the people attending your session.

Before you read on, take a moment and reflect on these situations and similar ones in which you've found yourself. What would you do? How did you handle the situation?

1. Make No Assumptions

Avoid making assumptions. For instance, do not assume people want to discuss a difficult topic. People may have already spent enough time discussing it and not view the training session as the appropriate time or place. Avoid assuming you know how people feel. There will be a variety of feelings. Avoid assuming you know all the details of a given situation. Most importantly, do not assume you can either solve the problem or change the way people are feeling. Remember: You are there to teach a workshop that has specific learning outcomes. Ask yourself: "What do I need to do to stand the best chance of achieving those objectives and make the most productive learning environment?"

2. Create an Open Environment of Trust and Vulnerability

In order for people to feel comfortable sharing what's on their minds, we must make them feel safe. If the group does not know you, this can be a real challenge. You have very little time to create an open environment. In all likelihood you will have to find a genuine way of demonstrating some vulnerability and sensitivity with the group. A short personal story well told and well timed can be very effective. For example, in the first situation from above you might tell a short anecdote of a recent experience that made you feel powerless, like a humorous but poignant customer service encounter. The combination of humor, frustration, and the similarities of an emotional experience that will resonate with their own is likely to loosen up a group. Don't forget that our nonverbal gestures are as important as anything we say. Try, as best you can, to be confident to act and speak extemporaneously. Be careful of pre-canned speeches and behaviors: They have the danger of coming across as hollow and insincere.

3. Validate Emotions

Find ways to validate people's feelings. There is a natural inclination to question feelings, probe for reasons why those feelings are there in the first place, or to offer explanations; however, none of these well-intentioned interventions help the situation. Even negative emotions can be transformed into potentially positive perceptions if we honor people's feelings. If you feel you have enough skill as a facilitator, try to get people to speak more from their hearts, emotions, and imaginations than from their heads.

4. Poll the Group

Here's a technique for getting a quick gauge on a group's feelings. Ask everyone to take a piece of paper and write down an adjective or two that describes how he or she is currently feeling. Collect all the pieces of paper and read the words out loud. You can also capture words on a flip chart. This has two clear benefits. First, it allows people to express their feelings in a safe way. Second, people will realize others have similar feelings. This can be a great way to lead into a discussion or decide to forego one, depending on the type of responses you receive.

5. Be Flexible with Your Timeline

Training sessions are never long enough. Allocating time to topics other than those on the agenda is likely to get you in time trouble. If you decide to tackle a sensitive topic, be prepared to give it enough time. Find other places in the agenda where you can cut. As long as you manage expectations and let people know that certain items on the agenda will not be covered, most people will not have a problem with the changes. Be sure to point out the value of the discussion and if possible relate it in some way back to the session's learning objectives.

6. Be Opinion-Less

While it is important to establish vulnerability with a group, we must be careful to leave our opinions and strong ideas at the door. Take the time to be self-aware of your own feelings prior to a session. During the session, watch and observe your own feelings but be careful of how you expose them. Remember: Whatever processing of emotions and discussion that might ensue during a session is for the participants and not for you. This is not to say that you should never bring your ideas or opinions to the group, but do so with utmost care, caution, and respect for the group and its needs.

Dealing with difficult issues in training is not easy stuff, nor can we follow any ready-made formula for how to deal with them, but responsibly leading a group through difficult issues is one of the most rewarding, humbling, and deepening experiences we can have as trainers.

Tips for Handling Challenging Learner Behaviors

Contributed by Shawn Scheffler

Note that this item specifies dealing with challenging "behaviors." Be careful of falling into the trap of calling learners themselves "difficult." Trainers sometimes have unrealistic expectations that learners will completely leave their homes and work lives outside the classroom. A distracted learner may have a sick child at home, or be worried about a looming deadline. Or learners may have legitimate reasons for being unhappy about the training itself. Perhaps they were sent to the training against their will and feel like "prisoners." Or maybe they do, in fact, know it all and need to have their expertise validated. Or perhaps they are bored, which may indicate that the problem is not with the learner but with the training design.

A last thought: While there is ample literature on dealing with difficult behaviors, there is little available on preventing problems in the first place. There are a number of proactive steps available to trainers. For instance: Send pre-course communication clearly outlining the content and goals of the program, so learners know what to expect; involve supervisors in training design so they can better decide which training is appropriate for which staff. Find out as much as possible about the learner group in advance, so you will know whether there are any employees with famously challenging behaviors enrolled and whether members have had unpleasant experiences with the topic before. For the present, however, here are quick tips for handling some challenging behaviors.

Seven Strategies for Addressing the Angst

- **Ignore the person.** Walk away from the source.

- **Stand near the person.** Present near the source (do not make contact).

- **Make eye contact.** Let the person know you are aware.

- **Identify the type.** Use the person in a hypothetical situation that the audience and the challenging learner can recognize.

- **Separate.** Create new group arrangements to get them out of a "comfort zone."

- **Take a break.** Let everyone escape a potential situation and meet with the contrary person in private.

- **Ask the person to leave.** If possible, discreetly ask him or her to leave, but don't let the audience lose any more time.

Adjust Your Interaction, Depending on the Learner's Intent

The Challenger—The Know-It-All

- Confirm the person's position (or disposition).

- Probe for details (asking for proof).

- Parse the issue.

- Counter with facts, but do not engage in an argument.

- Agree in part or agree to disagree.

- Redirect the person's comments and questions to the group.

The Dominator—Won't Shut Up

- Jump in, summarize, and relay.

- Make eye contact and move toward another person.

- Call on another person/expert to interject.

- Don't embarrass the person.

- Give the person something to do, for instance, make him or her a scribe during exercises.

The Side-Talkers—Constant Chit Chat

- Make eye contact and ask a question.

- Ask a question across the talkers.

- Ask "Can everyone hear alright?" without making eye contact.

- Be completely silent until they realize the transgression.

The Insecure One—Hello, Are You in There?

- Respond to non-verbal cues.

- Ask a question related to his or her experience.

- Don't force the person into the limelight.

- Reinforce any contribution.

Trainer Self-Preservation and Self-Development

The life of a trainer, particularly one who must travel or frequently work in different training rooms, can be exhausting. Even those trainers fortunate enough to have administrative support often find that their day is spent not only in delivering instruction, but in confirming registrations, locating training space, monitoring pre-work, keeping up with materials and equipment, and managing follow-up activities, all while meeting the needs of different learners. This section includes some survival tools for trainers: a basic checklist for keeping up with the materials relevant to a particular class; a more detailed checklist for those who must additionally deal with reserving rooms, scheduling speakers, working with caterers, and managing printing and other costs; a worksheet for communicating with guest speakers; a planner specifically designed for offsite training; and tips for managing the stress unique to the training profession. The last item offers suggestions for the "Lone Ranger Trainer," the person who serves as an organization's only trainer.

Tool 64. Training Logistics Action Items

Contributed by Results Through Training
(www.RTTWorks.com)

Here is a basic to-do list for managing a classroom training event.

❑ Supplies Identified/Ordered	❑ Trainer Travel Arrangements
❑ Confirm Attendance Number	❑
❑ Pre-Work Shipped	❑
❑ Training Reinforcement Guides	❑ Feedback Surveys, etc.
❑ Assignment Memo	❑
❑ Course Materials/Master to Production	❑ *Receipt Confirmed, Date:*
❑ Workbook	❑ Planner (and Cover?)
❑ Handouts	❑ Session Evaluation
❑ Action Plan (and Cover?)	❑
❑ *Binder Assembly*	
❑ Tabs for Wkbk	❑ Diskette Reproduction/Label
❑ Wkbk Cover and Slipcard/Spine	❑
❑ Course Materials to Hotel/Client	❑ *Receipt Confirmed, Date:*
❑ Pre-Work Compiled	❑
❑ Trainer Materials Shipped	❑ *Receipt Confirmed, Date:*
❑ Intro	❑ Flip Charts (slip cases Y/N, pp._____)
❑ Course Description	❑ Overhead Master
❑ Potential Icebreakers	❑ Overhead Transparencies
❑ Learning Environment Suggestions	❑ Key Words
❑ Milestone Checklist	❑ Quotes
❑ Preparation/Packing Checklist	❑ Tent Cards
❑ Room Setup	❑ Tabs/Trainer Kit
❑ Course Map	❑ Trainer Handouts/Answer Keys
❑ Course Materials	

❑ Masters	❑ Feedback Summary Reports and Master
❑ Agenda	
❑ Trainer Notes	❑ Directions to Hotel/Class
❑ Flip-Chart Master	❑ Trainer Evaluation Form
	❑ Learning Environment Props

❑ Facility Setup List to Hotel/Client	❑ *Receipt Confirmed, Date:*
❑ Deliv Aides (OH, F/C, toys) Shipped	❑ *Receipt Confirmed, Date:*

❑ Course FU to Client and Instructor

❑ F/C Transcribed; Draft to Instructor	❑ Follow-Up Letters
❑ Session Evaluations	❑ Certificates
❑ Distribution List Updated	❑

❑ Material Cleanup/Filing

❑ Computer Files Organized/Cleaned Up	❑ Material Masters Filed
❑ Flip Charts Cleaned/Stored	❑ Class Materials Unpacked/Filed/Logged

❑ Invoicing

Tool 65. Training Program/Activity Worksheet

Contributed by Bob Teague

This worksheet, courtesy of the San Francisco Area AIDS Education and Training Center, is a comprehensive tool for scheduling rooms, reserving equipment, planning catering, printing, and speaker budgeting. (And a reminder to send thanks to the speakers!)

PROGRAM INFORMATION	
Program/Activity Title:	
Day(s)/Date(s):	
Time/Duration:	
Program ID # (*from database*):	Is this a repeating program? ☐ Yes ☐ No
Location/Room:	Program Type: (*check all that apply*) ☐ Scheduled Training ☐ Special Request Program
Address/Directions:	☐ In-Service ☐ Conference ☐ Meeting/Event ☐ Workshop ☐ Faculty Development ☐ Satellite Broadcast
Course Director(s):	
Key Staff/Contact:	

Additional Key People:	Name/Program	Involvement	E-Mail	Phone #	FAX #
Co-Sponsor:					
Co-Sponsor Address:					

SPACE RESERVATIONS			
☐ Yes ☐ No Conf. Date:	Total # People: Site Fee(s): $	Site Contact: Phone #: ☐ Classroom ☐ U-Shape ☐ Theatre Seating ☐ Podium ☐ Speaker's Table ☐ Registration Table ☐ Catering Table(s) ☐ Chairs only	

Discipline	CE Program ID#	Provider Contact Info	App Fee	Cert Fee	Date Application Filed:

☐ CE Applications   ☐ CE Request Forms/Check Sheets   ☐ Budget Statements
☐ Commercial Support Statements
☐ Disclosure Statements   ☐ Course Outline and Objectives
☐ Needs Assessment Data

REGISTRATION

Registration Begins/ Closes:	/	Registration Fee? ☐ Yes ☐ No	Pre-Registration Required? ☐ Yes ☐ No
Min/Max # of Participants:	/	Fee Amount: $	Total Guarantee (# people):

☐ Confirmation Letter   ☐ Reminder Calls/Postcards   ☐ Maps/Directions

☐ On-site Registration

☐ Name Badges   ☐ Attendance Roster   ☐ CE Sign-In Sheet   ☐ Syllabus/Learner Materials

PROMOTION

☐ Yes ☐ No	Target Audience:			
☐ Announcement Date to Printer: Date Mailed:	# Mailed:	☐ Mailing Labels Source/Contact/Cost:		☐ Registration Flyer ☐ Poster Flyers ☐ Posted on Web ☐ CE Requirements
	Postage Cost: $			
	Printing Cost: $			
☐ Brochure/Flyer Date to Printer: Date Mailed:	# Mailed:	☐ Mailing Lists Source/Contact/Cost:		☐ Targeted Promotion ☐ Co-Sponsor Dist.
	Postage Cost: $			
	Printing Cost: $			
☐ FAX Broadcast:	FAX Broadcast Contact:			

A/V EQUIPMENT REQUISITION

Set up? ☐ Yes ☐ No   *Tech Support Phone:*

	#	Item	#	Item	#	Item
☐ Ordered:		LCD Projector		TV/VCR		Table Mic
		Slide Projector		Flip Chart		Floor Mic
☐ Confirmed:		Overhead Projector		Extension Cord		Lavalier Mic
Total A/V Costs: $		Screen		Cart		Wireless

MATERIALS

☐ Supplies Ordered (Date):		☐ Agenda/Objectives	☐ Handouts	**Guidelines:**	☐ JAFPB Tx Article
Total Supplies Cost: $		☐ PIF/PAETC Eval ☐ Course/CE Eval	☐ Maps/Directions ☐ Restaurant Listings	☐ Adult ARV ☐ Pediatric ARV	☐ PEP ☐ HCW Infection Control
☐ Syllabus to Printer (Date):		☐ Eval return envelope	☐ CE Information	☐ Perinatal ☐ O/I Preventionv	☐ Counseling and Testing
Total Syllabus Printing Cost: $		☐ Pre/Post-Test	☐ NCCC Brochure	☐ Hep C	☐ Drug Intx Tables/Guides ☐ OTHER:

CATERING

Set up? ☐ Yes ☐ No	Vendor Name/Contact:			Phone #:	FAX #:	
☐ Ordered:	☐ Breakfast	Time:	Type/Menu:			Cost: $
☐ Confirmed:	☐ AM Break	Time:	Type/Menu:			Cost: $
Total Costs: $	☐ Lunch	Time:	Type/Menu:			Cost: $
Notes:	☐ PM Break	Time:	Type/Menu:			Cost: $
	☐ Dinner/Reception	Time:	Type/Menu:			Cost: $

EXPENSE RECAP

Item	Amount	Item	Amount	Other:	
Meeting Room Charges		Syllabus/Materials—Supplies		Other:	
Catering Charges		Syllabus/Materials—Printing		**Total Other:**	
A/V Equipment Rental/Fees		**Total Syllabus/Materials Costs**		**Total Facility:**	
		CME Application Fee		**Total Promotional:**	
Total Facility Costs		Other CE Application Fees		**Total Syllabus:**	
Promotional Printing		**Total CE Fees**		**Total CME/CE:**	
Promotional Postage		Guest Faculty Travel		**Total Faculty:**	
		Guest Faculty Honoraria		**Total Other:**	
Total Promotional Costs		**Total Guest Faculty Expenses**		**TOTAL EXPENSES:**	

Speaker Info	Confirmation	Speaker Packet	A/V Requirements
	☐ Confirmed _____ ☐ Speaker Fee $_____ ☐ Travel ☐ Lodging ☐ Thank You _____	☐ Packet Sent_____ ☐ Objectives/Outline ☐ C/V ☐ Disclosure ☐ Syllabus Materials ☐ Consent to record: Y/N	☐ LCD Projector *Needs laptop? Y/N* ☐ Overhead ☐ Slide Projector ☐ TV/VCR ☐ Flip Chart ☐ Microphone ☐ Other:
	☐ Confirmed _____ ☐ Speaker Fee $_____ ☐ Travel ☐ Lodging ☐ Thank You _____	☐ Packet Sent _____ ☐ Objectives/Outline ☐ C/V ☐ Disclosure ☐ Syllabus Materials ☐ Consent to record: Y/N	☐ LCD Projector *Needs laptop? Y/N* ☐ Overhead ☐ Slide Projector ☐ TV/VCR ☐ Flip Chart ☐ Microphone ☐ Other:
	☐ Confirmed _____ ☐ Speaker Fee $_____ ☐ Travel ☐ Lodging ☐ Thank You _____	☐ Packet Sent _____ ☐ Objectives/Outline ☐ C/V ☐ Disclosure ☐ Syllabus Materials ☐ Consent to record: Y/N	☐ LCD Projector *Needs laptop? Y/N* ☐ Overhead ☐ Slide Projector ☐ TV/VCR ☐ Flip Chart ☐ Microphone ☐ Other:

	❏ Confirmed
	_____
	
	❏ Speaker Fee
	$_____
	
	❏ Travel
	❏ Lodging
	❏ Thank You
	_____
		❏ Packet Sent_____
		❏ Objectives/Outline
		❏ C/V ❏ Disclosure
		❏ Syllabus Materials
		❏ Consent to record:
		   Y/N
			❏ LCD Projector
			   Needs laptop? Y/N
			❏ Overhead
			❏ Slide Projector
			❏ TV/VCR
			❏ Flip Chart
			❏ Microphone ❏ Other:

Tool 66. Speaker/Presentation Information Worksheet

Contributed by Bob Teague

This worksheet serves as communication between the course organizer and the speaker.

Speaker/Presentation Profile Sheet

Please complete the profile below to ensure we have all the information about your presentation and your audiovisual equipment needs. You may return the completed form by (1) saving the completed it as a Microsoft Word document and e-mailing it to _____,; (2) faxing it to XXX-XXX-XXXX; (or 3) mailing to _____. We must receive the completed form by close of business on _____.

Session Description

Please provide a 75-to-150-word overview of your program. This will be used in the program marketing materials, brochures, agendas, etc., so please be clear about what you will cover, the approach (i.e., "hands-on seminar").

Learning Objectives

Please provide three specific learning objectives. These should inform the audience as to what they are to learn and what they are expected to do with the information you present.

Presentation Materials and Formats

Please provide electronic copies of your slides and/or handouts. You can submit these via CD by sending them to _____ or by emailing them to _____. We will print copies of your handouts to be included in participant packets.

Logistics

Parking: A facility map and directions are enclosed. Please check in with the receptionist at the front desk; a parking pass will be there for you.

Speaker/Session Profile

Program/Event	
Date:	
Location:	

Presenter Information

Name of Primary Presenter:	
Title:	
Organization:	
Degree(s):	
Mailing address:	
Best daytime phone:	
Email:	

Will you be co-presenting? If so, please provide names, titles, organizations, and degrees for other presenters.

Session Information

Title:	
Format (check all that apply):	_____ Lecture _____ Discussion _____ Case Study Roundtable _____ Clinic _____ Other (Describe: _____)
Equipment Needs	_____ LCD Projector/Laptop _____ Overhead Projector _____ Whiteboard _____ Flip Chart/Markers/Paper _____ TV/DVD _____ Internet Connection Phone Line
Other needs?	
Release:	

May we post your slides and handouts on our website? yes_____ no_____

Session Description

Please provide a 75-to-150-word overview of your session.

Learning Objectives

Please provide three learning objectives for your session.

Submit completed form to:

(email)   (FAX)

(address)

Tool 67. Trainer's Planner for Offsite Training

Contributed by Colette Haycraft

Working offsite means that everything, from the access code for a copier to the location of light switches, is an unknown. Here is a planning tool to help manage the special challenges for trainers working on the road.

One Week Before Class	
❑ Verify course date, time, and location	❑ Contact site coordinator to confirm
❑ Visit site if you have never trained there	❑ Find out what resources are available at site
❑ Speak with A/V and/or IT support staff	❑ Determine layout and capacity of room
❑ Confirm registered participants	❑ Confirm and secure available equipment
❑ Identify environmental controls (heat, air)	❑ Test unfamiliar equipment
❑ Send/Email class registration reminders	❑ Inquire about local food sites/shopping

One Day Before Class	
❑ Prepare certificates of completion	❑ Load backup information on CD or Flash
❑ Contact site coordinator one more time	❑ Have hard copy back-up information ready
❑ Prepare training agenda and handouts	❑ Make copies and extra copies of handouts
❑ Deliver supplies to training site today	❑ Pack up Trainer's Kit
❑ Get phone numbers of A/V or IT staff	❑ Email class registration reminders

Day of Class	
❑ Arrive as early as facility will allow	❑ Set up participant seating supplies
❑ Contact site coordinator and A/V or IT staff to let them know you are on-site	❑ Test all equipment, i.e., computers, printers, projectors, microphones
❑ Post appropriate signs for class	❑ Set up area for signing in
❑ Provide a "Parking Lot" for questions	❑ Provide and discuss evaluations
❑ Discuss "Housekeeping" of class site	

After Class	
❑ Be available for additional questions	❑ Return all equipment to proper place
❑ Make sure the room looks the same as when you arrived	❑ Pack up your Trainer's Kit
❑ Keep the "Parking Lot" to capture notes	❑ Check out with site coordinator
Personal Care	
❑ Glasses/contacts/accessories	❑ Aspirin/Tylenol/Advil
❑ Water bottle/coffee cup/thermos	❑ Cell phone number for other trainers
❑ Lunch/snack	❑ Toothbrush/breath freshener
❑ Tissues	❑ Travel umbrella
❑ Personal inspiration	❑ Briefcase/satchel w/Training Plan, etc.
❑ Emergency sewing kit	
Trainer's "Ready-for-Anything" Kit	
❑ Ream of paper	❑ Laser pointer
❑ Box of sharpened pencils	❑ Stapler/tape/paper clips
❑ Color markers/highlighters	❑ Rewards/giveaways
❑ Monitor wipes	❑ Labels/Post-it Notes
❑ 3 × 5 cards for questions/comments	❑ CD/memory stick/disk w/presentation
❑ Trainer Manual	❑ Sign-in sheets
❑ Icebreakers/brain teasers	❑ Scissors
❑ Public domain music	❑ Manual timer
❑ Toys	❑ Extra batteries, bulbs, cords
Other Necessary Resources/Items	
❑ Flip Charts	❑ Graphs
❑ Dry Erase Markers/Eraser	

Trainer Self-Preservation: Five Ideas for Taking Charge of Your Recharging

Contributed by Terrence Gargiulo

Trainers can be very susceptible to becoming stressed and overtired, and it's easy to burn out or get caught in a rut. Here are ideas for staying energized.

1. Watch Another Trainer

We all have distinct personalities and styles. It can be refreshing and insightful to watch a colleague at work. Be sure to drop your filter of comparison. The point is not to validate your techniques or affirm your worth as a trainer, but rather to bask in the energy and uniqueness of someone else. Make a point of acknowledging specific traits, characteristics, and techniques. Then resolve to try to incorporate some of what you observed in future sessions of your own.

2. Try Something New

How often do you try something new? Familiarity breeds comfort, predictability, and confidence, but a pearl would never be created without a good grain of sand. Trying new things in a session makes it exciting for trainers and puts us a bit on edge. There is nothing like a little sense of the unknown to add spice to our sessions and rev up our energy. It could be as simple as explaining a concept in a new way, introducing a new workshop or exercise, or changing the order in which you present topics. Whatever you do is bound to alter the tried and true. The results are sure to surprise you.

3. Read a Book on Training

A book can vicariously transport our imaginations to new vistas. Leisurely strolling through the thoughts of an author, especially one who's a fellow trainer, opens our minds to new possibilities. Thought experiments lead to new behavior and new behaviors can invigorate our sometimes-tired training routines. Tool 68 offers a list of highly recommended books for trainers, so consider starting there. Call a colleague and see what he or she is reading or recommends. Retreat to the pages of a book and start recharging.

4. Tackle a New Topic

When was the last time you facilitated something totally new? In order to be effective trainers, we need to be versatile and relentless learners. Greet a new challenge head on. Even if a new topic will not be one of your core ones, it will still give you a boost. It may also give you fresh ideas or approaches to topics that you facilitate on a regular basis. I remember having to fill in for another trainer at the last minute. I was absolutely petrified. I had virtually no knowledge or experience facilitating workshops on problem solving and critical thinking. I dove right into the material; absorbing anything and everything I could get my hands on. In the process I gained new confidence in my abilities as a facilitator, greater understanding of a new topic, and a whole new domain of knowledge that I was able to incorporate into my other workshops.

5. Rest

Everything has a rhythm and everything needs to be given the proper space to rebound and grow. We are not always the makers of our schedules, nor do we always have the luxury of time, but be sure to find little ways to increase whatever opportunity you have for rest.

Tool 68. Best Books for Trainers

Along with my requests for items for this book, I asked a number of contributors to send the title of their favorite book for trainers. Note the distinction: not necessarily books about training, but books for trainers. Most are, indeed, about training. But some, like Covey's 7 Habits of Highly Effective People, *are resources for building credibility and effectiveness regardless of profession. Another, Gawande's* Complications, *is an excellent first-person reflection of how an adult learns.*

Barbazette, J. (2003). *Instant case studies.* San Francisco, CA: Pfeiffer.

Berieter, C. (2002). *Education and mind in the knowledge age.* Mahwah, NJ: Lawrence Erlbaum Associates.

Bozarth, J. (2005). *e-Learning solutions on a shoestring: Help for the chronically underfunded trainer.* San Francisco, CA: Pfeiffer.

Bozarth, J. (2008). *Better than bullet points: Creating engaging e-learning with PowerPoint.* San Francisco, CA: Pfeiffer.

Brinkerhoff, R., & Apking, A. (2001). *High-impact learning.* New York: Perseus.

Cameron, E. (2005). *Facilitation made easy: Practical tips to improve meetings and workshops* (3rd ed.). London: Kogan Page.

Clark, R., & Lyons, C. (2005). *Graphics for learning: Proven guidelines for planning, designing and evaluating visuals in training materials.* San Francisco, CA: Pfeiffer.

Clark, R., & Mayer, R. (2002). *e-Learning and the science of instruction.* San Francisco, CA: Pfeiffer.

Clark, R., Nguyen, F., & Sweller, J . (2006). *Efficiency in learning: Efficiency-based guidelines to manage cognitive load.* San Francisco, CA: Pfeiffer.

Covey, S. (1999). *The 7 habits of highly effective people.* New York: The Free Press.

Driscoll, M., & Carliner, S. (2005). *Advanced web-based training strategies.* San Francisco, CA: Pfeiffer.

Ertmer, P., & Quinn, J. (2002). *Case studies in instructional design* (2nd ed.). Upper Saddle River, NJ: Pearson Education.

Gawande, A. (2003). *Complications.* New York: Picador.

Kapp, K. (2007). *Gadgets, games, and gizmos for learning: Tools and techniques from transferring know how from boomers to gamers.* San Francisco, CA: Pfeiffer.

Kruse, K., & Keil, K. (2000). *Technology-based training.* San Francisco, CA: Pfeiffer.

Laird, D. (1985). *Approaches to training and development.* Reading, MA: Addison-Wesley.

Lawson, K. (2006). *Trainer's handbook* (2nd ed.). San Francisco, CA: Pfeiffer.

Lee, W., & Owens, D. (2000). *Multimedia-based instructional design.* San Francisco, CA: Pfeiffer.

Mayer, R. (2001). *Multimedia learning.* New York: Cambridge University Press.

Meier, D. (2000). *The accelerated learning handbook: A creative guide to designing and delivering faster, more effective training programs.* New York: McGraw-Hill.

Morrison, G., Ross, M., & Kemp, J. (2001). *Designing effective instruction* (3rd ed.). Hoboken, NJ: John Wiley & Sons.

Newstrom, E., & Scannell, E. *The games trainers play* series from McGraw-Hill; assorted years. New York: McGraw-Hill.

Palmer, P. (1997). *The courage to teach.* San Francisco, CA: Jossey-Bass.

Phillips, J., & Stone, R. (2001). *How to measure training results : A practical guide to tracking the six key indicators.* New York: McGraw-Hill.

Piskurich, G. (2006). *Rapid instructional design: Learning ID fast and right.* San Francisco, CA: Pfeiffer.

Rosania, R. (2001). *The credible trainer: Create value for training, get respect for your ideas, and boost your career.* Alexandria, VA: ASTD Press.

Rosenberg, M. (2001). *e-Learning: Strategies for delivering knowledge in the digital age.* New York: McGraw-Hill.

Rossett, A., & Gautier-Downes, J. (1991). *A handbook of job aids.* San Francisco, CA: Pfeiffer.

Schank, R. (2005). *Lessons in learning, e-learning, and training.* San Francisco, CA: Pfeiffer.

Shank, P., & Sitze, A. (2004). *Making sense of online learning.* San Francisco, CA: Pfeiffer.

Silberman, M. (2005). *101 ways to make training active* (2nd ed.). San Francisco, CA: Pfeiffer.

Stolovitch, H., & Keeps, E. (2002). *Telling ain't training.* Alexandria, VA: ASTD/ISPI.

Toth, T. (2004). *Technology for trainers.* Alexandria, VA: ASTD.

Wenger, E., McDermott, R., & Snyder, W. (2002). *Cultivating communities of practice.* Boston, MA: Harvard Business School Press.

Wick, C., Pollock, R., Jefferson, R., Flanagan, R., & Wilde, K. (2006). *The six disciplines of breakthrough learning: How to turn training and development into business results.* San Francisco, CA: Pfeiffer.

Zemke, R., & Kramlinger, T. (1982). *Figuring things out: A trainer's guide to needs and task analysis.* Reading, MA: Addison-Wesley.

Zull, J. (2002). *The art of changing the brain.* Sterling, VA: Stylus.

Tips for the Lone Ranger Trainer

Contributed by Patti Shank, Cindy Epps, and Jane Bozarth

All this talk about training departments and staffs of evaluators and developers is great. But what if you are the organization's only designated training officer?

- Develop subject-matter experts into trainers and let them train. (Adequate is better than not at all, sometimes.)

- Make training everyone's job.

- Work on top priorities, not on fads that come down the pike.

- Patti Shank's secret weapon (don't tell): Start a project that is very valuable to the organization and top management and, when they ask to expand it, explain the resources that will be needed to do more.

- Tap into a network of other trainers.

- Cultivate the right relationships. Middle managers and your "end-user" learners can be your best friends.

- Join local chapters of the American Society for Training and Development and the International Society for Performance Improvement to get ideas from others.

- Understand the business so you can more easily prioritize.

- Get to know the decision makers in your organization.

- Tap into a network of other trainers.

- Find out about community resources for offering training in your organization. For instance, area hospitals often provide stop-smoking and weight loss clinics and CPR training.

- Google yourself silly.

- Attend workshops on trainer development and training program management.

- And . . . tap into a network of other trainers.

Things They Don't Tell You in Train-the-Trainer Courses

Submitted by Patti Shank, Cindy Epps, Jane Bozarth, Susan E. Nunn, Elizabeth Grimes, and Jennifer Hofmann

- Sometimes the learners know more than you do.

- Your job isn't to be the star, but to make the learners shine.

- It's ok not to be perfect.

- Always *always* arrive early.

- If you don't love training, find another line of work.

- Don't make flight plans assuming your session will end on time.

- Find someone who has taught the class before and take him or her to lunch—your treat.

- People don't argue with their own data: Get your learners to generate answers and solutions.

- As a trainer, you have an incredible opportunity to positively influence the entire organization. You can do this in a couple of ways. Model in the classroom what you want to see transferred to learners' performance. And work to build effective relationships throughout the organization that enable you, through a training role, to have a positive impact on the culture of your organization.

- Ask for comments, not questions.

- There *is* such a thing as a stupid question. Your job is to act as if it's not.

- Don't blame your content. There is no boring training, only boring trainers.

- Beware the Four-Letter Acronym and Any Approach Involving Furry Little Creatures: Training and management fads and gimmicky approaches waste money, time, and energy, and ultimately undermine the credibility of the training department. Work with management to identify real needs and effective solutions.

- One of the hardest skills is breaking people into small groups. It requires both math and communicating that math to others. Asking twenty people to "get into five groups" is not the same as asking them to get into "groups of five." Not being clear about this can cause a 5-minute disruption, rattle you, and annoy your participants.

- Good platform skills are necessary, but insufficient. If you are just an entertainer with no real understanding of the realities of the job, people will dismiss you. (And they should.)

- Understand your audience. Different audience types need a different approach. The formality, dress, and level of familiarity you might use with a group of Federal Bureau of Investigation agents might be different from what you would use with a group of youth counselors.

- Deal with reality: Plenty of breaks, nothing boring in the afternoon, lots of time for questions.

- You'll often have someone in class who wants to prove you wrong.

- Expect learners to expect to leave early.

- Be ready for the mid-afternoon slump—inject energy and activities.

- Be prepared for something to go wrong.

- Always take an extension cord, tape, and an extra set of markers.

- You must train the supervisor/manager to solve systems and attitudes, because supervisors/managers affect and control systems and attitude.

- Find and develop your unique training style.

- If what you're doing isn't working, try something else.

Additional Suggested Resources

This book is meant to be a compilation of tools and tips and therefore does not include specific experiential learning activities such as team-building exercises and icebreakers. There are literally dozens of books on the theme of "activities for trainers." An excellent starting place is the second edition of Mel Silberman's *101 Ways to Make Training Active* (Pfeiffer, 2005), which offers far more than 101 ideas for increasing learner engagement with and interest in training content.

CHAPTER 5

Evaluate

"Evaluation" as we usually hear it discussed in training circles really means summative data—the training is over and it is time to assess and rethink. Did the training accomplish its objectives? Can learners perform as desired? As this book is organized according to the ADDIE model, it makes sense to include all the evaluation tools here. But don't overlook the opportunities for formative, as-you-go evaluation and piloting rather than wait to conduct an "evaluation by autopsy" after the fact. Also, as noted in Chapter 2: Design in the discussion of creating objectives, the best way to ensure that training achieves the desired outcomes is to begin with the end in mind. Being clear and specific about desired outcomes will support the success of the training effort.

This chapter offers tools and tips for both formative and summative evaluation, with those in the latter category broken out by evaluator: client, trainer, and learner. Several variations of the familiar "smile sheet" form are included. There is additional discussion of, and tools for, approaches to evaluation. The most familiar is the four-level (reaction, acquisition, application, and impact) Kirkpatrick taxonomy, which seeks to measure outcomes; another approach, the Stufflebeam CIPP (context, input, process, and product), model is also offered here as a mechanism for evaluating not just for results but also for improvement.

Formative evaluation is the chef tasting the soup while there's still time to make adjustments.

Summative evaluation is the food critic's review of the soup.

Lockee, B, Moore, M. & Burton, J. (2002). Measuring Success: Evaluation strategies for distance education. *Educause Quarterly, 1,* 20–26.

Formative Evaluation

Formative evaluation examines the effectiveness of program elements as they are being *formed* and allows for immediate revision or quick intervention. It is entirely focused on improvement and maximizing the likelihood that the training will achieve its intended outcome. It is much easier to catch, and fix, a problem as training is being developed, particularly if it comes to light that planned activities or approaches are not meeting the training objectives as expected. You have already seen some formative evaluation tools corresponding to their respective phases of the ADDIE process, such as Tool 36: Fink's Principles of Good Course Design, Tool 49: Evaluation Worksheet for Graphic Treatment; and Tool 61: Training Design Checklist: Comprehensive Version.

Tool 69. Formative Self-Evaluation Tool

I have found this an excellent tool, easily adaptable to any topic, for encouraging learner reflection, self-assessment, and ownership of new learning. It is also a good way for trainers to assess the learners and the program and adjust the instructional plan as necessary. While it is presented here as a tool for using with a whiteboard in a virtual classroom session, it would work equally well as a paper instrument.

Instructions: I originally developed this tool for use in a synchronous online workshop for trainers new to teaching virtually. At the beginning of the first class, I ask learners to rate themselves on their level of competence/skill at training online ("ready"), their belief that this approach can be "as good as" the traditional classroom experience ("willing"), and their assessment of their organization's readiness to utilize virtual classroom approaches to training—the trainer's ("able") ability to deliver training to the organization's workforce. I provide it on the synchronous product's whiteboard and ask learners to use the text tool to place themselves on each continuum. We can then discuss where people feel they are. The exercise ends by asking them to set their own goals for the course and create an action plan for achieving them. I save the whiteboard.

Later in the course—prior to the last session, while there's still time to address remaining concerns—I display the whiteboard from the first session, showing them where they initially placed themselves, and ask the learners to again rate themselves. As before, this opens the door to conversation about remaining needs, emerging issues, and further action plans.

Course Day 1

Learners: Ann, Bob, Jane, Richard, Susan

The learners' assessments of themselves (see Figure 5.1) show that most, except for Bob, are "willing" but few feel they currently have the skills to be successful ("ready"). Jane feels she does not have complete organizational support ("able"). Learners discuss goals, changes they need to make, and action plans for overcoming barriers.

Figure 5.1. Rate Yourself: Day 1

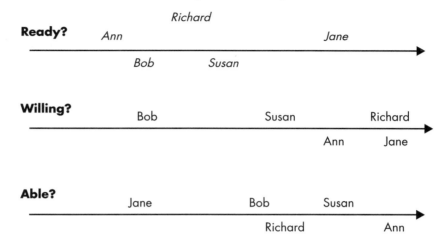

Rate yourself: Day 1

Course Day 5

Learners are presented with the screen from the earlier session—
including their own earlier ratings—and are again asked to assess
themselves (the new assessments are shown in Figure 5.2 in a bold
script font). All the learners feel they have increased their skills and are
competent to perform. Bob is much more willing, but Susan's self-
assessment of her "willingness" has changed little since Day 1, so this
may be something worth exploring. Richard's assessment of "able"— the
support of his organization—has decreased considerably; on probing,
he reveals that the course developed his awareness of the importance of
a producer to support synchronous training sessions, and he is concerned that his organization will not agree to this additional expense.

Figure 5.2. Rate Yourself: Day 5

Rate yourself: Day 5

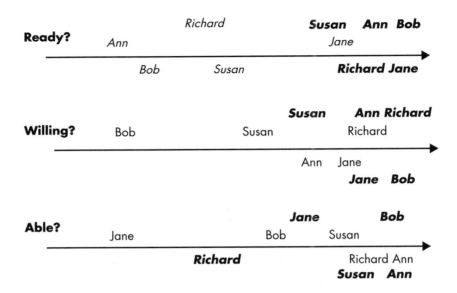

Tool 70. Course Daily Reflection

While this tool was designed for use in a multi-day program, it could be edited for use as an activity for learners returning from lunch during a single-day class. The trainer can ask that the completed forms be turned in, either anonymously or with names, to see what learners felt was especially meaningful, and to ensure that what struck learners as especially important is aligned with the course goals. It can also be valuable to see what, and whether, learners intend to try and use back on the job.

Yesterday we covered:

Something (s) that really struck me as interesting, new, provocative, challenging, meaningful was/were:

One change I will make, as a result of yesterday, to my ongoing practice in the workplace:

Tips for Formative Evaluation

During the Design and Development Phases

- Do test-runs of planned activities, pilot test, and quiz items.

- Were examples adequate and explanatory information clear?

- Get different perspectives. Run ideas and materials by subject-matter experts.

- One of the best, but least-utilized, sources of formative information comes from the ultimate end-users: the learners. Include them in analysis, design, and development activities.

- Use Tools 36, 49, 59, 60, and 61 to evaluate your work in progress.

During Pilot-Training Sessions

- Talk with learners at breaks about what they feel they've learned.

- Use Tool 70: Course Daily Reflection to gather feedback.

- Give short quizzes or require short demonstrations or "teachbacks" during the program.

- Are the trainers competent in delivering the material?.

- Is timing adequate for each activity? Is the trainer so busy "pushing content" that the program seems rushed?.

- Is the interaction among participants and between instructor and facilitator adequate? Use Tool 62: Mapping Discussion Flow to help inform this.

- Have an outside observer sit in on pilots to take notes. Observe learners: What questions are they asking? Pay attention to learner questions. Is there anything that could "trip up" learners? Is terminology adequately defined? Are instructions written clearly enough that learners can complete an activity on the first try, without having to ask for clarification or additional information?

- Develop a community of people you trust to give honest, constructive feedback.

Throughout

- Ask yourself: Did we identify the learner needs correctly?

- Ask yourself: Are the objectives meaningful and realistic?

- Be open to feedback. Listen, don't defend.

Summative Evaluation: Client, Team, and Trainer Evaluation of Training

While the most common form of training program evaluation is the learner "smile sheet" or reaction form, other participants and stakeholders attached to training design project can also provide valuable information. This section includes tools for gathering data from clients, design team members, and the trainers who conduct the training sessions.

Tool 71. Post-Mortem: Client's Evaluation of Training Project

Contributed by Patti Shank

This project evaluation form is used to solicit client input at the completion of a project. Developer Patti Shank uses this form to frame a meeting or conference call to discuss results and implications for future projects.

Questions	Score 1 To 5 (1 = Lowest; 5 = Highest)	Comments
Project team. How would you rate the team that worked on this project? Notable strengths and weaknesses?		
Project management. Did you feel confident that the project was well managed? What problems occurred? Were they resolved to your satisfaction?		
Communication. Are you satisfied with how team members communicated with you? Were you able to communicate openly with them? How could communication be improved?		
Responsiveness and commitment. Were team members accessible and responsive to you and your needs and concerns? Were they committed to desired project outcomes?		
Lessons learned. What should be done differently to ensure fewer problems and better results in the future?		

Questions	Score 1 To 5 (1 = Lowest; 5 = Highest)	Comments
Rate the overall project/ results from A to F. Why did you rate it this way?		
Recommendations. Would you work with this team on another project? Recommend them to others?		
Additional comments? Is there anything we didn't ask but should know about?		

For each of the listed people/groups, please describe:		
Team Member	**Positive Impact(s) on Project Outcomes**	**Ways the Person Could Improve on Future Projects**

Tool 72. Post-Mortem: Team's Evaluation of the Training Project

Contributed by Michael Greer (www.michaelgreer.com)

*It's important to take stock at the end of a project and develop a list of lessons learned so as to capture successful activities and avoid making the same mistakes next time. This tool, originally designed for project management applications, works well for reviewing training projects. Contributor Michael Greer recommends a two-step process for conducting these reviews: individuals first work alone to generate answers from their own points of view, then meet as a group to share their responses. Note that the questions do not ask only "Are you **satisfied** with our products, deliverables, and results?," but whether team members are **proud** of them. While targeted at a team, the questions are equally provocative for the "lone ranger" trainer.*

Instructions

First, prepare specific questions about the project and give team members time to think about them and prepare their responses individually.

Next, hold a meeting and discuss the team's responses to the questions. The result of this discussion is often a list of "Lessons Learned."

The benefit of the first step, done individually by team members, is that it allows the quieter, more analytical people to develop their responses to the questions without being interrupted by the more outgoing, vocal types who might otherwise dominate in the face-to-face meeting. Also, it allows everyone the time to create more thoughtful responses.

Here are suggestions for the types of questions that might be asked:

General Questions

1. Are you proud of our finished deliverables (project work products)? If yes, what's so good about them? If no, what's wrong with them?

2. What was the single most frustrating part of our project?

3. How would you do things differently next time to avoid this frustration?

4. What was the most gratifying or professionally satisfying part of the project?

5. Which of our methods or processes worked particularly well?

6. Which of our methods or processes were difficult or frustrating to use?

7. If you could wave a magic wand and change anything about the project, what would you change?

8. Did our stakeholders, senior managers, customers, and sponsor(s) participate effectively? If not, how could we improve their participation?

Phase-Specific Questions

(These will differ from project to project, depending on the life cycle/phases.)

Phase I: Analyze

1. Did our needs analysis identify all the deliverables that we eventually had to build? If not, what did we miss and how can we be sure our future analyses don't miss such items?

2. Did our needs analysis identify unnecessary deliverables? If so, how can we be sure our future analyses don't make this mistake?

3. How could we have improved our needs analysis phase?

Phase II: Design

1. How accurate were our original estimates of the size of and effort required for our project? What did we over- or under-estimate? (Consider deliverables, work effort, materials required, etc.)

2. How could we have improved our estimate of size and effort so that it was more accurate?

3. Did we have the right people assigned to all project roles? (Consider subject-matter expertise, technical contributions, management, review and approval, and other key roles.) If no, how can we make sure that we get the right people next time?

4. Describe any early warning signs of problems that occurred later in the project. How should we have reacted to these signs? How can we be sure to notice these early warning signs next time?

5. If applicable: Could we have completed this training effort without one or more of our vendors/contractors? If so, how?

6. If applicable: Were our constraints, limitations, and requirements made clear to all vendors/contractors from the beginning? If not, how could we have improved our RFP or statement of need?

7. If applicable: Were there any difficulties negotiating the vendor contract? How could these have been avoided?

8. If applicable: Were there any difficulties setting up vendor paperwork (purchase orders, contracts, etc.) or getting the vendor started? How could these have been avoided?

9. List team members or stakeholders who were missing from initial planning or who were not involved early enough in our project. How can we avoid these oversights in the future?

10. Were all team/stakeholder roles and responsibilities clearly delineated and communicated? If not, how could we have improved these?

11. Were the deliverables specifications, milestones, and specific schedule elements/dates clearly communicated? If not, how could we improve this?

12. Were you proud of our blueprints or other detailed design specifications? If not, how could we have improved these?

13. Did all the important project players have creative input into the creation of the design specifications? If not, who were we missing and how can we assure their involvement next time?

14. Did those who reviewed the design specifications provide timely and meaningful input? If not, how could we have improved their involvement and the quality of their contributions?

15. How could we have improved our work process for creating deliverables specifications?

Phase III: Develop

1. Were you proud of our deliverables? If not, how could we have improved these?

2. Did all the important project players have creative input into the creation of the deliverables? If not, who were we missing and how can we assure their involvement next time?

3. Did those who reviewed the deliverables provide timely and meaningful input? If not, how could we have improved their involvement and the quality of their contributions?

4. How could we have improved our work process for creating deliverables?

Phase IV: Implement

1. Were the members of our pilot audience truly representative of our target learners? If not, how could we assure better representation in the future?

2. Did the pilot facilities, equipment, materials, and support people help to make the pilot an accurate representation of how the program will be used in the "real world"? If not, how could we have improved on these items?

3. Did we get timely, high-quality feedback about how we might improve our deliverables? If not, how could we get better feedback in the future?

4. Was our implementation strategy accurate and effective? How could we improve this strategy?

5. Did our hand-off of deliverables to the user/customer/sponsor represent a smooth and easy transition? If not, how could we have improved this process?

Phase V: Evaluate

1. Were you proud of our evaluation methods? If not, how could we have improved these?

Tool 73. Trainer's Evaluation of Session/Learners

Contributed by Randy Woodward

From contributor Randy Woodward: "Being a trainer myself, I understand that the learner evaluations don't always tell the whole story, so I designed the facilitator feedback form to put evaluation of a session into a more holistic context. Additionally, it gives the trainer a chance to reflect on the experience from his or her own point of view—something we may otherwise skip, being busy with the next task. I am also a training manager and, from that perspective, the completed form, submitted by trainers on my staff, provides me the opportunity to put myself in their shoes and look for signs of stress, issues with systems like registration and marketing (Are we getting the right people in the right class?), and of course to find opportunities to praise good performance. Plus, if others who may be unfamiliar with the class, trainer, or learners (like C-level staff) review the training report, they get a more balanced view of the intent and the results.

"Finally, the form helps to answer questions like, 'Why did this group only show a 2 percent improvement in skills?' Maybe they attended a class that was three levels below their current skills, or perhaps learners were scheduled to attend directly following a twelve-hour shift and hadn't slept for a day and a half. Or perhaps they were sent to training in an effort to remediate a character flaw that has nothing to do with a knowledge or skill deficiency. None of these is likely to show up in the learner feedback, but the trainer will usually know, and should really have a chance to document that and communicate it to management. Finally, it gives a place for the facilitator to identify people we want to invest in: star performers and folks who show potential for future development."

Session/Workshop: _____   Date(s):_____

Location: _____   Trainer(s): _____

Attitude: 5   4   3   2   1   0   1   2   3   4   5
       Positive   Mixed   Negative

Mood: (circle all that apply) ☐ Focused   ☐ Fun   ☐ Rowdy   ☐ Happy   ☐ Bored
                            ☐ Angry   ☐ Confrontational   ☐ Tired/Sleepy   ☐ Other____

Receptiveness to Concepts: 5   4   3   2   1   0   1   2   3   4   5
             Eager to Learn   Neutral   Total Rejection

Attention Level: 5   4   3   2   1   0   1   2   3   4   5
        High   Neutral   Low

Preparation: (Learners knew what knowledge and skills the session was designed to convey, what kind of activities to expect, what the trainer would expect from them, and/or had prepared *appropriate* learning goals/objectives for themselves)

5   4   3   2   1   0   1   2   3   4   5
High   Neutral   Low

Participation: 5   4   3   2   1   0   1   2   3   4   5
      Eager   Active   Moderate   Reluctant   None

Attendance: ☐ Much Higher   ☐ Higher   ☐ As Scheduled   ☐ Lower   ☐ Much Lower

Level of Material: (for this group)   ☐ Too Easy   ☐ Just Right   ☐ Too Hard

Appropriateness of Material: (for this group)

5   4   3   2   1   0   1   2   3   4   5
Highly   Moderately   Not
Applicable   Applicable   Applicable

Makeup of Learners:

_____ % Learners (appeared to want to be here, interested in learning)

_____% Vacationers (appeared to attend freely but not taking training very seriously)

_____% Prisoners (appeared to be—or stated that they were—forced to attend)

_____% Not sure

Additional Comments:_____

_____

_____

_____

_____

_____

_____

_____

_____

_____

_____

_____

_____

_____

Summative Evaluation: Learner Evaluation of Training

It seems there are as many variations on learner "smile sheet" or reaction forms as there are trainers; most ask, in one way or another, for similar data. Here are three sample forms: one asking primarily for numerical responses, one asking for written comments, and one requesting more in-depth information about a particular program.

Tool 74. Learner Course Evaluation Template A: Overview

Contributed by Jennifer Henczel

Here's a course evaluation form with an interesting twist: learners create and evaluate some items of their own. This is brought to us by Jennifer Henczel at www.importexportcoach.com.

Course Evaluation				
Date:		**Location:**		
Please take some time to reflect over your opinions about today's session. Place a check mark in the box that best represents your response to the workshop characteristics being evaluated.				
The Workshop . . .	**strongly agree**	**agree**	**disagree**	**strongly disagree**
1. Increased my understanding of import/export.	☐	☐	☐	☐
2. Handouts and resources were useful.	☐	☐	☐	☐
3. Content was relevant to my current situation.	☐	☐	☐	☐
4. Visual presentation helped me to learn..	☐	☐	☐	☐
5. Length of time was adequate.	☐	☐	☐	☐
6. Assignments helped me to learn.	☐	☐	☐	☐
7. _____ (Create your own item and rate it)	☐	☐	☐	☐
8. _____ (Create your own item and rate it)	☐	☐	☐	☐
The Instructor . . .	**strongly agree**	**agree**	**neutral**	**strongly disagree**
9. Clearly explained workshop concepts.	☐	☐	☐	☐
10. Effectively organized workshop activities.	☐	☐	☐	☐
11. Provided a variety of learning activities.	☐	☐	☐	☐
12. Created an atmosphere conducive to learning.	☐	☐	☐	☐
13. Treated me with respect.	☐	☐	☐	☐
14. _____ (Create your own item and rate it)	☐	☐	☐	☐
15. _____ (Create your own item and rate it)	☐	☐	☐	☐

Please circle the point along the scale that best represents your response to the characteristic being valued.

16. I would recommend this **workshop** to others.

5	4	3	2	1
Yes				No

I gave this rating because. . .

17. I would recommend this **instructor** to others.

5	4	3	2	1
Yes				No

I gave this rating because . . .

18. I am interested in attending other workshops.

5	4	3	2	1
Yes				No

Please place a check in the box beside the topics that you are interested in, and add your own suggestions in the blanks provided)

☐ Advanced International Business Communications		☐ Developing Effective International Marketing Plans	
☐ Top 100 International Trade Websites		☐ Advanced Importing Strategies	
☐ Working in the U.S.		☐ Advanced Exporting Strategies	
☐ International Marketing		☐ Logistics and Customs Documentation	
☐		☐	

19. Overall, I would like to add . . .

Tool 75. Learner Course Evaluation Template B: Narrative

Contributed by Linda Levine

This form requests more written information from learners, and explicitly asks about the intent to apply the material back at the workplace.

Course Title: _____   Date: _____

Overall, how would you rate this course? (circle your rating)

Excellent _____ Poor

           1   2   3   4   5

Rate Your Knowledge and Skill Level (circle your rating)

Before this course: Low _____ High

                   1   2   3   4   5

After this course Low _____ High

                  1   2   3   4   5

Describe Your Three Key Insights from this training session.

1.

2.

3.

Strong Points of the Course:

Weak Points of the Course:

Additional Information You Would Like to Have Covered in Course:

Was There Any Unnecessary Material?

Would You Recommend This Course to Other Employees? Why or Why Not?

I Will Share What I Learned with Others in My Organization in the Following Ways:

Tool 76. Learner Course Evaluation Template C: Detailed

Created by the North Carolina Justice Academy; modified and contributed by Malea Drew

This is a more extensive evaluation instrument. The example below shows its use in evaluating an annual train-the-trainer course, providing detailed questions about the quality of materials, the organization's use of the materials and program content, and the worth of course prerequisites.

Topic: 2007 Train-the-Trainer Course

Trainer: _____   Date: _____

How might the course be improved?

Any suggestions for future training?

Please rate the following statements: Key: SD = Strongly Disagree D = Disagree N = Neutral A = Agree SA = Strongly Agree	SD	D	N	A	S
CONTENT					
1. The course objectives were clear.	O	O	O	O	O
2. The course objectives agree with the material covered in class.	O	O	O	O	O
3. Topics covered were relevant to course objectives.	O	O	O	O	O
4. The course content met all the stated objectives.	O	O	O	O	O
5. The content was clear.	O	O	O	O	O
6. The procedures were clear.	O	O	O	O	O
7. The level of information available suited my needs as a trainer.	O	O	O	O	O
8. The course length was sufficient.	O	O	O	O	O
MATERIALS					
9. The course participant materials (handouts, manuals, etc.) were useful in class.	O	O	O	O	O
10. Participant materials were appropriate for the course topic.	O	O	O	O	O
11. The materials were clear and easy to follow.	O	O	O	O	O
12. The depth and breadth of course materials were adequate.	O	O	O	O	O
13. I'll be able to refer to the materials for follow-up support.	O	O	O	O	O
14. The CD-ROM worked properly.	O	O	O	O	O
15. The CD-ROM was helpful.	O	O	O	O	O
PERFORMANCE IMPROVEMENT					
16. My knowledge or skill level has increased.	O	O	O	O	O

17. Which describes you?
  O Ten years or more of experience
  O Fewer than ten years of experience		

	Yes	**No**
18. Did you use the following materials from the 2007 Train-the-Trainer course?		
a. Instructor lesson plan	O	O
b. Student lesson plan	O	O
c. Instructor handout	O	O
d. Student handout	O	O
e. PowerPoint presentation	O	O
f. Videos embedded in the PowerPoint presentation	O	O

Please rate the following statements: Key: SD = Strongly Disagree D = Disagree N = Neutral A = Agree SA = Strongly Agree	SD	D	N	A	SA
19. The following materials from the 2007 Train-the-Trainer course were useful to the instructor:					
a. Instructor lesson plan	O	O	O	O	O
b. Student lesson plan	O	O	O	O	O
c. Instructor handout	O	O	O	O	O
d. Student handout	O	O	O	O	O
e. PowerPoint presentation	O	O	O	O	O
f. Videos embedded in the PowerPoint presentation	O	O	O	O	O
20. The following materials from the 2007 Train-the-Trainer course were useful to the <u>class</u>:					
a. Student lesson plan	O	O	O	O	O
b. Student handout	O	O	O	O	O
c. PowerPoint presentation	O	O	O	O	O
d. Videos embedded in the PowerPoint presentation	O	O	O	O	O
21. The material provided in the 2007 Train-the-Trainer can adequately prepare a trainer for his or her role as a presenter.	O	O	O	O	O

	Yes	No
22. Did you attend the 2006 (last year) Trainer Update?	O	O
a. If yes, was the information from the 2006 Trainer Update helpful to your presentation in understanding the material?	O	O
b. If yes, was the information from the 2006 Trainer Update helpful to your presentation in presenting the material?	O	O
23. Did your agency conduct more than two hours of training?	O	O
24. Did your agency teach the optional review?	O	O
25. Did your agency supplement the two hours with additional instruction?	O	O
26. How many training sessions did you conduct?		
27. How many students did you teach? *(total number approximately)*		

Course and Program Evaluation

While learner reaction is a common form of program evaluation, and important, it is only the beginning of a solid evaluation process. This section includes tools for conducting a more thorough evaluation and discusses the familiar evaluating for improvement as well as results.

Tool 77. Strategies for Evaluating Training Results

Contributed by Dr. John Sullivan

Dr. John Sullivan, of performance culture and identifying metrics fame, offers these guidelines for evaluating training. He is one of the few to note the value of pre-training evaluation strategies.

Prior to Training

- The number of people who say they need it during the needs analysis process.

- The number of people who sign up for it.

At the End of Training

- The number of people who attend the session.

- The number of people who paid to attend the session.

- Customer satisfaction (learners) at end of training.

- Customer satisfaction at end of training when customers know the actual costs of the training.

- A measurable change in knowledge or skill at end of training.

- Ability to solve a "mock" problem at end of training.

- Willingness to try or intent to use the skill/knowledge at end of training.

Delayed Impact (Non-Job)

- Customer satisfaction at X weeks after the end of training.

- Customer satisfaction at X weeks after the training, when customers know the actual costs of the training.

- Retention of knowledge at X weeks after the end of training.

- Ability to solve a "mock" problem at X weeks after end of training.

- Willingness to try (or intent to use) the skill/knowledge at X weeks after the end of the training.

On-the-Job Behavior Change

- Trained individuals who self-report that they changed their behavior/used the skill or knowledge on the job after the training (within X months).

- Trained individuals whose managers report that they changed their behavior/used the skill or knowledge on the job after the training (within X months).

- Trained individuals who actually are observed to change their behavior/use the skill or knowledge on the job after the training (within X months).

On-the-Job Performance Change

- Trained individuals who self-report that their actual job performance changed as a result of their changed behavior/skill (within X months).

- Trained individuals whose managers report that their actual job performance changed as a result of their changed behavior/skill (within X months).

- Trained individuals whose managers report that their job performance changed (as a result of their changed behavior/skill), either through improved performance appraisal scores or specific notations about the training on the performance appraisal form (within X months).

- Trained individuals who, have observable/measurable (improved sales, quality, speed, etc.) improvement in their actual job performance as a result of their changed behavior/skill (within X months).

- The performance of employees who are managed by (or are part of the same team with) individuals who went through the training.

- Departmental performance in departments with X percent of employees who went through training ROI (cost/benefit ratio) of return-on-training dollar spent (compared to our competition, last year, other offered training, preset goals etc.).

Other Measures

- CEO/Top management knowledge of/approval of/or satisfaction with the training program.

- Rank of training seminar in forced ranking by managers of what factors (among miscellaneous staff functions) contributed most to productivity/profitability improvement.

- Number (or percent) of referrals to the training by those who have previously attended the training.

- Additional number of people who were trained (cross-trained) by those who have previously attended the training and their change in skill/behavior/ performance.

- Popularity (attendance or ranking) of the program compared to others (for voluntary training programs).

The Kirkpatrick Taxonomy for Evaluating Training Programs

The first, and still best-known, structured approach to measuring training results is the four-level taxonomy introduced by Donald Kirkpatrick in 1959. The levels are, in order:

1. Learner reaction/satisfaction (usually measured by "smile sheets" similar to those provided in Tools 74, 75, and 76)

2. Learner demonstration of understanding (i.e., passing a test)

3. Learner demonstration of new skills or behaviors on the job

4. The impact these new skills or behaviors (hence, the training) has on the workplace

Jack Phillips later added a fifth level, return on investment (ROI), which seeks to measure the cost savings and "bottom line" results to the organization by measuring the costs associated with the training from the benefits it generated.

What Is "ROI"?

Those seeking to measure the return on investment, or ROI, of a training program are attempting to establish proof of the program's worth in financial terms. An attempt at evaluating ROI is typically undertaken in order to justify the expense of training to management and other stakeholders. The formula is very straightforward:

$$(\text{training benefits} - \text{training cost}) / \text{benefits} \times 100$$

Here's an example: if the training costs are \$100,000, and the benefits are determined to be \$200,000, then:

$$(\$200,000 - \$100,000)/\$200,000 \times 100$$
$$= \$100,000/\$200,000 \times 100 = .5 \times 100$$

$$= 50\% \text{ return on the investment in training:}$$
for every dollar spent, \$1.50 was gained

But while the formula is straightforward, the matter of assigning a numerical value to "benefits" is often very difficult. If Factory X experiences a high rate of forklift-related accidents, provides critical safety training targeted at forklift operation, and sees an immediate drop in the accident rate, then it might be possible to correlate the training to savings in terms of workers' compensation payments, lost work hours, and perhaps fines by regulatory agencies. What about, however, quantifying the results of a "stress management" course? Or a program on "ethics in the workplace"? Or training in leadership skills? Tool 78 offers some suggestions for measuring programs at different levels in the Kirkpatrick taxonomy, but often the benefit value used in calculating ROI is just the subjectively assigned (by management or other stakeholders) financial worth of an intangible such as "increased loyalty" or "enhanced public perception of ethical behavior."

Another problem in establishing "ROI" is linking the training effort directly to an outcome. As discussed in more depth later in this chapter, there are many factors that may facilitate or inhibit learner performance subsequent to attending training, and attempting to isolate the effects of training from the system in which performance exists can be very, very difficult. Suppose a hospital, in an effort to reduce the spread of infections, implements a new, mandatory training program on hand washing. As part of this "initiative," the hospital simultaneously installs new wash stations, places containers of sanitizing hand gel in prominent locations, and orders hot-pink warning signs to put on the doors of patients with especially contagious types of infections. If the infection rate drops—or does not drop—what can be attributed directly to the training? How can the hospital separate the effects of the training from the other factors that may have had an impact? What if the rate has a noticeable drop on one floor of the hospital, but not another, even though all staff received the same training? Or, what if, in advance of a new product launch, a company invests in sending the entire sales force through "refresher" training on persuasive sales techniques. Six months later, sales figures on the new product are disappointing. Was the training investment wasted? Or could the problem be related to data that doesn't show up when using the Kirkpatrick taxonomy, such as marketing dropped the ball. There were abundant problems in the shipping process. Promised accessories for the new product were not made available on time.

One solution to the problem of isolating training from other factors is to use a control group (one group trained, one not), as suggested in the chart for Tool 78. Again, that may not work in all situations: the hospital likely won't want to risk a heightened infection rate while waiting months to determine the effectiveness of training with the control group. Stufflebeam's CIPP model, explained in Tool 79, makes room for examination of the contextual and other factors that may be related to the ultimate success of a training program.

As ROI is such a popular metric in the current training and human resources literature, it does bear mention in this book. While those interested in ROI might find it helpful to ask for expert help with an ROI undertaking, such as hiring experienced evaluation consultants, two tools will help you obtain the data you need for a simple "ROI" calculation of your own programs: use Chapter 2's Tool 29, the "Rule of Thumb" Costs for Training estimator, to calculate the expenses associated with your program, and Tool 78, Evaluating Training at Five Levels, the next item here, to establish monetary measures of results. Then apply the formula:

$$(\text{training benefits} - \text{training cost})/\text{benefits} \times 100.$$

Tool 78. Evaluating Training at Five Levels

Many organizations never go much beyond evaluation at Level 1 (learner reaction) and very few ever venture into attempting to measure ROI. This is partly due to the difficulty of establishing meaningful measures of "benefits," While it is a fairly straightforward process to measure the time spent on rework and assign a per-hour savings in terms of labor cost, it is considerably harder to quantify the value of, for instance, a "leadership" course, a class on workplace Spanish, or a workshop on PowerPoint basics. Below are some suggestions for measuring several example programs at all five levels.

Topic	Level 1: Satisfaction	Level 2: Knowledge/ Skill Gain	Level 3: On-the-Job Use	Level 4: Results	Level 5: ROI
General	Summative evaluation form that solicits learner reaction to the training; also known as "smile sheet" evaluations. Use one of the "Learner Course Evaluation" tools (Tool 74, 75, or 76)	Use a control group; use pre- and post-training assessments of knowledge, skills, or attitudes; conduct on-the-job assessments; solicit reports from supervisor; use results to take corrective actions	Use a control group; repeat evaluation periodically; allow time for change to occur; survey/review reports from customers, colleagues, and supervisors; learner self-assessment	Use a control group; allow time for results; find meaningful measures; define "results"; review documents such as financial reports, accident reports, and quality inspections; realize you may find "evidence" rather than "proof"	(A) Calculate monetary worth of benefits associated with the training, such as productivity increases, increased sales, reduced breakdown, turnover, complaint, or rework rates, reduced labor costs; (B) Calculate all costs associated with the training; design, marketing, materials, faculty, other staffing, administrative costs, costs associated with having learners out of the work setting, learner costs, evaluation costs, and facilities and equipment costs, subtract training costs (B) from benefits achieved (A)
Writing Skills	Use one of the "Learner Course Evaluation" tools (Tool 74, 75, or 76)	Compare pre- and post-workshop writing samples	Surveys of graduates' customers and colleagues soliciting comments on quality of post-workshop work	Measures such as productivity increases, changes in error and rewrite rates, etc., three to six months following training	Calculate monetary worth of changes in productivity and error and rewrite rates; solicit input from managers and other stakeholders to assign monetary worth of enhanced public image

Topic	Level 1: Satisfaction	Level 2: Knowledge/ Skill Gain	Level 3: On-the-Job Use	Level 4: Results	Level 5: ROI
Call Center: Mortgage Industry	Use one of the "Learner Course Evaluation" tools (Tool 74, 75, or 76)	Use control group; pre- and post-tests using customer situations	Using control group, monitor sampling of calls to assess performance of those trained compared to non-trained. (Establish criteria/checklist for assessing quality of managing calls.) ; follow-up surveys with customers, colleagues, and supervisors and, if applicable, others in communication or supply chain	Using control group, compare trained and non-trained groups on rates at which caller interest resulted in a closed mortgage; also measure and cross-measure sales levels for two, four, and six months following training to pre-training periods	Calculate worth of change in rates of closed mortgages; use sales figures in calculating benefits; calculate worth of repeat callers and callers who were referred by satisfied customer

Alternatives to Kirkpatrick?

While the Kirkpatrick taxonomy is something of a sacred cow in training circles—and much credit goes to Donald Kirkpatrick for being the first to attempt to apply intentional evaluation to workplace training efforts—it is not the *only* "formal" approach. According to some critics, the Kirkpatrick approach is flawed for evaluating everything after the fact, focusing too heavily on end results while gathering little data that will help inform training program improvement efforts. (Discovering after training that customer service complaints have not decreased only tells us that the customer service training program didn't "work"; it tells us little about how to improve it.) The linear causality implied within the taxonomy (for instance, the assumption that passing a test at Level 2 will result in improved performance on the job at Level 3) masks the reality of transfer of training efforts into measurable results. There are many factors that enable or hinder the transfer of training to on-the-job behavior change, including support from supervisors, rewards for improved performance, culture of the work unit, issues with procedures and paperwork, and political concerns. Learners work within a system, and the Kirkpatrick taxonomy essentially attempts to isolate training efforts from the systems, context, and culture in which the learner operates.

In the interest of fairness I would like to add that Kirkpatrick himself has pointed out some of the problems with the taxonomy and has suggested that in seeking to apply it the training field has perhaps put the cart before the horse. He advises working backward through his four levels more as a design, rather than an evaluation, strategy; that is: What business results are you after? What on-the-job behavior/performance change will this require? How can we be confident that learners, sent back to the work site, are equipped to perform as desired? And finally: How can we deliver the instruction in a way that is appealing and engaging?

An alternative approach to evaluation was developed Daniel Stufflebeam. His CIPP model, originally covering Context-Input-Process-Product/Impact, and later extended to include Sustainability, Effectiveness, and Transportability, provides a different take on the evaluation of training. Tool 79 offers more explanation and an example of the CIPP model in practice.

Tool 79. Stufflebeam's CIPP Model of Evaluation

As Stufflebeam's Context-Input-Process-Product model includes multiple stakeholders (learners, their co-workers and managers, customers, and even instructors), it is hoped that they will be inclined "to study, accept, value, and act upon evaluation findings" (Stufflebeam, 2003, p. 13), supporting the ultimate goal of the use of evaluation data towards improvement. The CIPP model is flexible, allowing for fluidity and overlap between the phases, rather than the lockstep approach forced by the Kirkpatrick taxonomy. It is also, as shown in the example here, useful for evaluating an entire training program—in this case, the organization's distance learning program—rather than a single class.

Following are the elements examined in the CIPP Model:

Context seeks information to help situate the evaluation study and includes a review of items, such as company/program history, current events, and organization culture.

Input examines program resources and assets.

Process examines what is actually happening as well as what should be happening but is not.

Product/Impact seeks to identify specific program outcomes, both intended and unintended.

Sustainability asks how well the program is embedded in the organization's overall operations.

Effectiveness examines how far-reaching the outcomes are and asks, "Who was served by this program?"

Portability asks whether the program is replicable. How easily could it be adopted by another work unit or organization?

Here's an example of the CIPP model in action, using the example of the ACME Corporation's request for an evaluation of the effectiveness of their distance education program.

Context involves seeking information to help situate the study and the place of the distance education program. This phase could include methods such as surveys, document and archive review, stakeholder interviews, focus groups, and the review of training materials and lesson plans.

- What is Acme's history? Why did Acme implement the distance education program? For example, was Acme seeking to reduce classroom training costs, increase the reach of training efforts, or better meet compliance requirements?

- What was the intended target audience, and why?

- How would Acme define the "success" of the program? Increased enrollments, increased completions, or some evidence that distance learning efforts are being transferred to the work setting?

- Is there also a traditional classroom-based program, and if so, why is the distance program viewed as distinctly separate?

- What political issues are involved? Who are the program's champions and adversaries, and why?

- How was the program introduced? How were the trainers chosen, and what preparation did they receive? Were the trainers previously classroom trainers? Were they previously Acme classroom trainers?

Input is an examination of program resources. These include measures surrounding staffing, numbers of learners, budget, costs of technology/equipment/learning management system/technology support. Methods for assessing at this phase would include activities such as reviewing cost analysis, review of documentation surrounding issues such as staffing and equipment, and comparison of the program under review to similar programs offered by Acme's competition.

- Are there salary issues or monetary rewards connected to the situation of the trainers working in the distance education program?

- Is the budget sufficient for the intended goals?

- What supplemental materials are available to learners, such as a company library or journal subscriptions?

Process examines the ways activities are carried out and seeks to assess both what actually is happening as well as what *should* be happening but is not. Acme's extant data relative to internal or informal program evaluation—learner reaction sheets, feedback from learners, test scores, certifications—should be examined. A model of assessing trainer skills, such as guidelines based on Chickering and Gamson's (1987) principles for effective practice could be incorporated within this phase. Additional methods could include surveys, interviews, observations, case studies, focus groups, data related to faculty preparation, record of program events, problems, costs, allocations, and technology/registration systems/ access issues.

- What is the quality of technical support and effectiveness of learner and trainer preparation efforts?

- What are trainer perceptions of the program and its effectiveness?

- Are there organizational or cultural factors enabling or prohibiting performance, good or bad?

- What feedback or support are trainers given?

- What are the professional activities of the trainers? Are they part of a community of practice? Is reflection encouraged? What kind of feedback do they receive beyond learner reaction evaluations?

- Additional means of assessment specific to the quality of online instruction, such as the IHEP benchmarks, could be applied (elements missing from the IHEP literature but present in other guidelines, such as measures of sustainability and trainer satisfaction, exist elsewhere in the CIPP model.)

Product, or impact, is an examination of direct program outcomes. This includes both intended and unintended outcomes and asks questions such as those listed below. Methods could include surveys, focus groups, review of documentation of items such as enrollment and completion rates, test scores, comparison to other programs, observation, and case studies.

- Is Acme achieving important outcomes? Are those outcomes congruent with stated needs?

- Are enrollment numbers and completion rates in line with targets?

- Are there any trends in staff turnover related to the distance education program?

- What are the basic knowledge, skills, and abilities gained by learners?

- What are learner perspectives of impact?

- What happens once learners return to the work site? Are there factors enabling or hindering behavior change on the job?

- What happens to learners subsequent to program completion? Is completion tied to promotional opportunities or pay increases?

- What are learner and trainer perceptions of impact, not only reaction or satisfaction to the program, but whether they feel the program brings any result?

Effectiveness is an examination of the Acme distance education program's farther-reaching outcomes. Methods at this phase might include surveys, document review, comparison to other programs, assessment of what the program actually did, case studies of selected beneficiaries, and documentation on the range, depth, quality, and significance of program's effects on beneficiaries.

- Is the program reaching the intended audience?

- Do enrollees represent non-target groups? Are the "right" people attending?

- Who was served by the program: learners, managers, work units, customers? Others? Are they the intended beneficiaries?

- What is the outcome for beneficiaries? Are learners promoted into new jobs? Do work units see changes in items such as error rates or accidents?

- How is the program influencing the "community" of the workplace?

Sustainability studies the degree to which the distance education program is embedded in Acme's overall operations. Methods would include surveys, observations, a review of Acme materials such as mission statement, brochures, website, and marketing material. Surveys and focus groups with stakeholders would include conversation about what to keep, what to eliminate, and what to revise or revisit.

- Is the program mentioned in mission statements, marketing materials, and other company documentation?

- Does it have a presence on Acme's website?

- What is management's official position on distance education as an approach and as a valued Acme program? In other words, is the program institutionalized?

- Should Acme desire it, this phase could also address staffing and budget forecasting.

Portability: The final step of the Acme evaluation would ask:

- Could the Acme program be adopted elsewhere?

- Can it serve as model for others?

Methods would include visits to other programs, interactions with stakeholders, logs of inquiries from "outside" inquiring about the program, visitors wanting to participate in the program or talk with designers/trainers, surveys or interviews with those wanting to adopt the program, and adaptations of the program made by other organizations with site visits to assess them.

References

Chickering, A., & Gamson, Z. (1991). *Applying the seven principles of good practice for undergraduate education.* San Francisco, CA: Jossey-Bass.

Stufflebeam, D.L. (1972). The relevance of the CIPP evaluation model for educational accountability. *SRIS Quarterly, 4*(1).

Stufflebeam, D.L. (1973). Evaluation as enlightenment for decision making. In B.R. Worthen & J.R. Sanders (Eds.), *Educational evaluation: Theory and practice.* Worthington, OH: Charles A. Jones Publishing.

Stufflebeam, D.L. (2003). The CIPP model for evaluation. Paper presented at the 2003 Annual Conference of the Oregon Program Evaluators Network (OPEN), Portland, Oregon.

Additional Suggested Resources

If you want to learn more about evaluation, start by searching the Web for big names and terms like Donald Kirkpatrick, Daniel Stufflebeam, and "training ROI," Well-known books on the subject include:

Ajzen, I. (1985). *From intentions to actions: A theory of planned behavior.* Heidelberg, Germany: Springer.

George, J., & Cowan, J. (1999). *Handbook of techniques for formative evaluation: Mapping the student's learning experience.* London: Kogan Page.

Hale, J. (2002). *Performance-based evaluation: Tools and techniques to measure the impact of training.* San Francisco, CA: Pfeiffer.

Kirkpatrick, D. (1998). *Evaluating training programs: The four levels.* San Francisco, CA: Berrett-Koehler.

Phillips, J. (1997). *Handbook of training evaluation and measurement methods* (3rd ed.). Houston, TX: Gulf.

As mentioned in the discussion of problems with the Kirkpatrick model, many factors affect the transfer of training to the workplace. Among these is learner intent. Tools 70 and 75 in this chapter ask learners to explicitly state how they intend to change their behavior or otherwise use the training back on the job. The theory of planned behavior holds that intent is critical to subsequent action; that is, the learner who does not *intend* to make use of the training likely will not. It is therefore important that the training, and the trainer, work to generate positive feelings toward the subject matter, compelling reasons to make the changes required to use new skills, and confidence that such use will be successful and worthwhile. There is a good deal of research-based literature on the theory of planned behavior and its underpinning, the theory of reasoned action, based on its application to educational endeavors as well as other fields in which persuasion of learners, customers, or clients is of special interest, such as advertising and health care. The earliest work on the subject is from the original theorist, Icek Ajzen. An Internet search for "theory of planned behavior" will provide dozens of sites offering basic information and links to further reading.

LIST OF CONTRIBUTORS

Teri Armstrong is training director for Catawba County, NC, USA, Human Services.

Jean Barbazette is president of The Training Clinic in Seal Beach, California, a training consulting firm she founded in 1977. She is a leading provider of train-the-trainer endeavors and a prolific author, with books including *Instant Case Studies* and *The Trainer's Journey to Competence*, both from Pfeiffer. See www.thetrainingclinic.com.

Pete Blair is a longtime trainer and course developer, and is presently director of customer training for DazzlerMax. See www.peteblair.com.

Susan Boyd is owner of Susan Boyd Associates, a Pennsylvania-based firm specializing in computer training. See www.susan-boyd.com.

Jane Bozarth is the e-learning coordinator for the state of North Carolina, USA, coordinator of the NC government training network, and author of *e-Learning Solutions on a Shoestring* and *Better Than Bullet Points: Powerful PowerPoint-Based e-Learning*. See www.bozarthzone.com.

Saul Carliner, Ph.D., assistant professor of educational technology at Concordia University, is author of *Advanced Web-Based Strategies* (with Margaret Driscoll) and *An Overview of Online Learning*.

Don Clark by day works for the Information Services/Inventory Control Department at Starbucks Coffee Company and by night helms the famous "Big Dog's" HRD and performance site www.nwlink.com/~donclark/index.html.

Ruth Clark specializes in evidence-based resources for design and development of classroom training and e-learning. She is the author, with Chopeta Lyons, of Pfeiffer's *Graphics for Learning*, and, with Richard Mayer, of Pfeiffer's *e-Learning and the Science of Instruction* (2nd ed.).

Nina Coil is director of product development and research for Linkage, Inc. www.linkageinc.com.

Ann Downer is executive director, International Training & Education Center on HIV (I-TECH), University of Washington, Seattle. See www .aids-ed.org/.

Malea Drew is a training specialist with the NC Justice Academy.

Cindy Epps, Mecklenburg County NC Human Services, is a member of the senior faculty for the NC Certified Training Specialist Program.

L. Dee Fink, Ph.D., is director of the Instructional Development Program at the University of Oklahoma and the author of *Creating Significant Learning Experiences: An Integrated Approach to Designing College Courses.*

Stephanie Freeman is an adjunct instructor for NC Wesleyan University.

Terrence Gargiulo is the author of several books, among them *Making Stories: A Practical Guide for Organizational Leaders and Human Resource Specialists* and *The Trainer's Portable Mentor.*

Michael Greer is a well-known project management expert, author, and speaker. See www.michaelgreer.com.

Elizabeth Grimes is manager of staff development and employee relations for the University of North Carolina at Wilmington.

Nancy Gustafson, Ed.D., is senior vice president of organization effectiveness at First Citizens Bank.

Jan Haverkamp oversees the Czech Republic's Zhaba facilitator's collective, meant to help facilitators develop skills and share talents. See www .zhaba.cz.

Colette Haycraft is a training specialist for the state of Delaware, USA.

Jennifer Henczel is a training practitioner and consultant specializing in helping clients with business start-up and moves into global markets. See www.jenniferhenczel.com.

Jennifer Hofmann, owner of InSync Training LLC, is an expert on synchronous training. She is the author of *The Synchronous Trainer's Survival Guide* and *Live and Online!* See www.insynctraining.com.

The **Honolulu Community College Faculty Development** organization is committed to providing support for faculty on instructional design and distance learning. See http://honolulu.hawaii.edu/intranet/

committees/FacDevCom/guidebk/online/online.htm and http://
honolulu.hawaii.edu/intranet/committees/FacDevCom/index.htm.

Anne Howard is a founding member and longtime leader of the NC
Training Network Team (TNT). Mission: "To stamp out bad training."

Anne Hull is president of Hull Strategies, LLC.

Karl Kapp, Ed.D., is the assistant director of Bloomsburg University's
Institute for Interactive Technologies and a professor of instructional
technology. He is the author of *Gadgets, Games and Gizmos for Transferring Know-How from Boomers to Gamers* and *Winning e-Learning Proposals*.
See www.karlkapp.com.

Kevin Kruse is an entrepreneur, author, and speaker in the field of
e-learning. He is the author of *Technology-Based Training* (Pfeiffer, 2000)
and other books, a columnist for *CLO* magazine and SPBT Focus, and is
the president of AXIOM Professional Health Learning. See his website
www.e-learningguru.com for articles and whitepapers on technology-
based training.

Gary Lear is president and CEO of Resource Development Systems, LLC:
www.rds-net.com/people.htm.

Linda Levine is the training coordinator for the North Carolina
Information Technology Services.

Jerry Linnins is senior manager for operational excellence at Genentech,
Inc.

Chopeta Lyons is an instructional designer and, with Ruth Clark, author
of *Graphics for Learning* (Pfeiffer).

Lenn Millbower is author of *Show Biz Training* (AMACOM) and *Cartoons
for Trainers* (Stylus).

Nanette Miner, Ed.D., is the author of *The Accidental Trainer* and owner
of training design and consulting firm The Training Doctor. See www
.trainingdr.com.

Susan E. Nunn is with the Cabarrus County, NC, Human Resources.
She is an executor.

Thomas Reeves, Ph.D., is a professor of educational psychology and
instructional technology at the University of Georgia. His contributions
originally appeared on a site hosted by Georgia Tech's College of
Sciences Center for Education Integrating Science, Mathematics, and
Computing. See http://www.ceismc.gatech.edu/mm_Tools.

Results Through Training, www.rttworks.com , is a Louisiana-based training and consulting firm. Materials here appear courtesy of RTTWorks President Colleen Orchanian.

Lou Russell is president and CEO of Russell Martin & Associates, a consulting and training company focusing on improving planning, process, and performance. She is the author of several books, including *The Accelerated Learning Fieldbook: Project Management for Trainers.* See www.russellmartin.com.

Peggy Schaefer is the director of the North Carolina, USA, Justice Academy.

Shawn Scheffler is Division 53 Training and Operations Manager for H & R Block.

Patti Shank owns Colorado-based Learning Peaks LLC training design firm, and is author of *The Online Learning Idea Book* and coauthor of *Making Sense of Online Learning.*

Lori Silverman is owner of www.partnersinprogress.com, author of *Wake Me Up When the Data Is Over,* and coauthor of *Stories Trainers Tell.*

Dr. John Sullivan is a well-known human resources consultant and speaker, and author of *Improving Productivity the World-Class Way* (Kennedy Information).

Bob Teague, MSW, is with the San Francisco Area AIDS Education and Training Center. See www.ucsf.edu/sfaetc.

Mitchell Weisberg is a founding partner of Academic Business Advisors LLC, www.academicbiz.com.

Randy Woodward is training and development director for Ho-Chunk Casino, Dells - Baraboo, Wisconsin.

Dan Young works in Standards Development, Interactive Courseware & Publications, Southeastern Computer Consultants, Inc. He can be contacted at instrudesign@gmail.com.

Jane Bozarth is an internationally known trainer, speaker, and author. A training practitioner since 1989, Jane is a graduate of the University of North Carolina at Chapel Hill, has an M.Ed. in training and development/technology in training from NC State University, and is presently finishing her doctorate in training and development. Jane's specialty, finding low-cost ways of creating or purchasing quality e-learning solutions, led to publication of *e-Learning Solutions on a Shoestring* and *Better Than Bullet Points: Powerful PowerPoint e-Learning* (both from Pfeiffer).

She enjoys business writing, and in addition to her regular column in *Training* magazine, Jane's work has appeared in trade and academic journals. She has contributed chapters to several other books, including the *2008 Pfeiffer Annual: Training*. Jane and her husband, Kent Underwood, live in Durham, North Carolina. She can be contacted via her website: www.bozarthzone.com.

HOW TO USE THE CD-ROM

System Requirements

PC with Microsoft Windows 98SE or later

Mac with Apple OS version 8.6 or later

Using the CD with Windows

To view the items located on the CD, follow these steps:

1. Insert the CD into your computer's CD-ROM drive.

2. A window appears with the following options:

Contents: Allows you to view the files included on the CD-ROM.

Software: Allows you to install useful software from the CD-ROM.

Links: Displays a hyperlinked page of websites.

Author: Displays a page with information about the Author(s).

Contact Us: Displays a page with information on contacting the publisher or author.

Help: Displays a page with information on using the CD.

Exit: Closes the interface window.

If you do not have autorun enabled, or if the autorun window does not appear, follow these steps to access the CD:

1. Click Start→Run.

2. In the dialog box that appears, type d:<\\>start.exe, where d is the letter of your CD-ROM drive. This brings up the autorun window described in the preceding set of steps.

3. Choose the desired option from the menu. (See Step 2 in the preceding list for a description of these options.)

In Case of Trouble

If you experience difficulty using the CD-ROM, please follow these steps:

1. Make sure your hardware and systems configurations conform to the systems requirements noted under "System Requirements" above.

2. Review the installation procedure for your type of hardware and operating system.

It is possible to reinstall the software if necessary.

To speak with someone in Product Technical Support, call 800–762–2974 or 317–572–3994 M–F 8:30 A.M.–5:00 P.M. EST. You can also get support and contact Product Technical Support through our website at www.wiley.com/techsupport.

Before calling or writing, please have the following information available:

- Type of computer and operating system

- Any error messages displayed

- Complete description of the problem.

It is best if you are sitting at your computer when making the call.

Pfeiffer Publications Guide

This guide is designed to familiarize you with the various types of Pfeiffer publications. The formats section describes the various types of products that we publish; the methodologies section describes the many different ways that content might be provided within a product. We also provide a list of the topic areas in which we publish.

FORMATS

In addition to its extensive book-publishing program, Pfeiffer offers content in an array of formats, from fieldbooks for the practitioner to complete, ready-to-use training packages that support group learning.

FIELDBOOK Designed to provide information and guidance to practitioners in the midst of action. Most fieldbooks are companions to another, sometimes earlier, work, from which its ideas are derived; the fieldbook makes practical what was theoretical in the original text. Fieldbooks can certainly be read from cover to cover. More likely, though, you'll find yourself bouncing around following a particular theme, or dipping in as the mood, and the situation, dictate.

HANDBOOK A contributed volume of work on a single topic, comprising an eclectic mix of ideas, case studies, and best practices sourced by practitioners and experts in the field.

An editor or team of editors usually is appointed to seek out contributors and to evaluate content for relevance to the topic. Think of a handbook not as a ready-to-eat meal, but as a cookbook of ingredients that enables you to create the most fitting experience for the occasion.

RESOURCE Materials designed to support group learning. They come in many forms: a complete, ready-to-use exercise (such as a game); a comprehensive resource on one topic (such as conflict management) containing a variety of methods and approaches; or a collection of like-minded activities (such as icebreakers) on multiple subjects and situations.

TRAINING PACKAGE An entire, ready-to-use learning program that focuses on a particular topic or skill. All packages comprise a guide for the facilitator/trainer and a workbook for the participants. Some packages are supported with additional media—such as video—or learning aids, instruments, or other devices to help participants understand concepts or practice and develop skills.

- *Facilitator/trainer's guide* Contains an introduction to the program, advice on how to organize and facilitate the learning event, and step-by-step instructor notes. The guide also contains copies of presentation materials—handouts, presentations, and overhead designs, for example—used in the program.

- *Participant's workbook* Contains exercises and reading materials that support the learning goal and serves as a valuable reference and support guide for participants in the weeks and months that follow the learning event. Typically, each participant will require his or her own workbook.

ELECTRONIC CD-ROMs and web-based products transform static Pfeiffer content into dynamic, interactive experiences. Designed to take advantage of the searchability, automation, and ease-of-use that technology provides, our e-products bring convenience and immediate accessibility to your workspace.

METHODOLOGIES

CASE STUDY A presentation, in narrative form, of an actual event that has occurred inside an organization. Case studies are not prescriptive, nor are they used to prove a point; they are designed to develop critical analysis and decision-making skills. A case study has a specific time frame, specifies a sequence of events, is narrative in structure, and contains a plot structure—an issue (what should be/have been done?). Use case studies when the goal is to enable participants to apply previously learned theories to the circumstances in the case, decide what is pertinent, identify the real issues, decide what should have been done, and develop a plan of action.

ENERGIZER A short activity that develops readiness for the next session or learning event. Energizers are most commonly used after a break or lunch to stimulate or refocus the group. Many involve some form of physical activity, so they are a useful way to counter post-lunch lethargy. Other uses include transitioning from one topic to another, where "mental" distancing is important.

EXPERIENTIAL LEARNING ACTIVITY (ELA) A facilitator-led intervention that moves participants through the learning cycle from experience to application (also known as a Structured Experience). ELAs are carefully thought-out designs in which there is a definite learning purpose and intended outcome. Each step—everything that participants do during the activity—facilitates the accomplishment of the stated goal. Each ELA includes complete instructions for facilitating the intervention and a clear statement of goals, suggested group size and timing, materials required, an explanation of the process, and, where appropriate, possible variations to the activity. (For more detail on Experiential Learning Activities, see the Introduction to the *Reference Guide to Handbooks and Annuals*, 1999 edition, Pfeiffer, San Francisco.)

GAME A group activity that has the purpose of fostering team spirit and togetherness in addition to the achievement of a pre-stated goal. Usually contrived—undertaking a desert expedition, for example—this type of learning method offers an engaging means for participants to demonstrate and practice business and interpersonal skills. Games are effective for team building and personal development mainly because the goal is subordinate to the process—the means through which participants reach decisions, collaborate, communicate, and generate trust and understanding. Games often engage teams in "friendly" competition.

ICEBREAKER A (usually) short activity designed to help participants overcome initial anxiety in a training session and/or to acquaint the participants with one another. An icebreaker can be a fun activity or can be tied to specific topics or training goals. While a useful tool in itself, the icebreaker comes into its own in situations where tension or resistance exists within a group.

INSTRUMENT A device used to assess, appraise, evaluate, describe, classify, and summarize various aspects of human behavior. The term used to describe an instrument depends primarily on its format and purpose. These terms include survey, questionnaire, inventory, diagnostic, survey, and poll. Some uses of instruments include providing instrumental feedback to group members, studying here-and-now processes or functioning within a group, manipulating group composition, and evaluating outcomes of training and other interventions.

Instruments are popular in the training and HR field because, in general, more growth can occur if an individual is provided with a method for focusing specifically on his or her own behavior. Instruments also are used to obtain information that will serve as a basis for change and to assist in workforce planning efforts.

Paper-and-pencil tests still dominate the instrument landscape with a typical package comprising a facilitator's guide, which offers advice on administering the instrument and interpreting the collected data, and an initial set of instruments. Additional instruments are available separately. Pfeiffer, though, is investing heavily in e-instruments. Electronic instrumentation provides effortless distribution and, for larger groups particularly, offers advantages over paper-and-pencil tests in the time it takes to analyze data and provide feedback.

LECTURETTE A short talk that provides an explanation of a principle, model, or process that is pertinent to the participants' current learning needs. A lecturette is intended to establish a common language bond between the trainer and the participants by providing a mutual frame of reference. Use a lecturette as an introduction to a group activity or event, as an interjection during an event, or as a handout.

MODEL A graphic depiction of a system or process and the relationship among its elements. Models provide a frame of reference and something more tangible, and more easily remembered, than a verbal explanation. They also give participants something to "go on," enabling them to track their own progress as they experience the dynamics, processes, and relationships being depicted in the model.

ROLE PLAY A technique in which people assume a role in a situation/ scenario: a customer service rep in an angry-customer exchange, for example. The way in which the role is approached is then discussed and feedback is offered. The role play is often repeated using a different approach and/or incorporating changes made based on feedback received. In other words, role playing is a spontaneous interaction involving realistic behavior under artificial (and safe) conditions.

SIMULATION A methodology for understanding the interrelationships among components of a system or process. Simulations differ from games in that they test or use a model that depicts or mirrors some aspect of reality in form, if not necessarily in content. Learning occurs by studying the effects of change on one or more factors of the model. Simulations are commonly used to test hypotheses about what happens in a system—often referred to as "what if?" analysis—or to examine best-case/worst-case scenarios.

THEORY A presentation of an idea from a conjectural perspective. Theories are useful because they encourage us to examine behavior and phenomena through a different lens.

TOPICS

The twin goals of providing effective and practical solutions for workforce training and organization development and meeting the educational needs of training and human resource professionals shape Pfeiffer's publishing program. Core topics include the following:

Leadership & Management

Communication & Presentation

Coaching & Mentoring

Training & Development

e-Learning

Teams & Collaboration

OD & Strategic Planning

Human Resources

Consulting

What will you find on pfeiffer.com?

• The best in workplace performance solutions for training and HR professionals

• Downloadable training tools, exercises, and content

• Web-exclusive offers

• Training tips, articles, and news

• Seamless on-line ordering

• Author guidelines, information on becoming a Pfeiffer Affiliate, and much more

Discover more at www.pfeiffer.com